JULIUS CAESAR

Adaptation by **James Butler and Maria Lucia de Vanna**
Activities by **Adeline Richards**
Illustrated by **Gianni De Conno**

Editor: Michela Bruzzo
Design and art direction: Nadia Maestri
Computer graphics: Emilia Coari
Picture research: Laura Lagomarsino

© 2000   Black Cat Publishing,
              an imprint of Cideb Editrice, Genoa, Canterbury

Revised edition
© 2007   Black Cat

Picture credits:
From the RCS Collection with the permission of the Governors of the Royal Shakespeare
Company: 4; www.visitlondon.com: 5; © Museo e Gallerie Nazionali di Capodimonte, Naples,
Italy, / The Bridgeman Art Library: 7-8; © Private Collection, Photo © Bonhams, London, UK /
The Bridgeman Art Library: 37; The British Museum, London: 39; © Araldo de Luca/CORBIS:
60; © David Ball/CORBIS: 61; © Jon Arnold Images / Alamy: 63; © Israel images / Alamy: 80;
© Bettmann/CORBIS: 81; © John Springer Collection/CORBIS: 84.

We would be happy to receive your comments and suggestions, and give you any other
information concerning our material.
info@blackcat-cideb.com
www.blackcat-cideb.com

CISQ CISQ CERT
TEXTBOOKS AND
TEACHING MATERIALS
The quality of the publisher's
design, production and sales processes has
been certified to the standard of
UNI EN ISO 9001

ISBN 978-88-530-0732-2   Book + CD

Printed in Italy by Litoprint, Genoa

Contents

The text is recorded in full.

These symbols indicate the beginning and end of the passages linked to the listening activities.

There are also extra listening activities downloadable from our website, www.blackcat-cideb.com or www.cideb.it. These activities correspond to tracks 5, 7, 9, 11, 13 and 15 on the Audio CD.

A portrait of **William Shakespeare** by an unknown artist. It is a copy made in the early 19th century of a portrait that was in the Folio edition of the plays of Shakespeare, which was published in 1623. This copy is called the **Flowers portrait** because it was owned by a family called Flowers.

The Life of
William Shakespeare

William Shakespeare was born in 1564 in Stratford-upon-Avon, a small town in central England. The exact date of his birth is not known, but many people like to believe that he was born on 23 April. This is St George's Day, the day of the patron saint of England.

William Shakespeare's father made and sold gloves. [1] He was involved in local politics in Stratford-upon-Avon, and became the town mayor. [2] It is likely that William Shakespeare was educated at the grammar school in Stratford-upon-Avon, where boys were taught Latin and Roman history.

When he was eighteen Shakespeare married Anne Hathaway, who was eight years older than himself. They had three children: a daughter, Susanna, and twins, Hamnet and Judith. Hamnet died young, at the age of eleven.

We do not know what Shakespeare did immediately after marriage, and there are a lot of stories about what have been called the 'missing years'. It is known,

1. **gloves** : you wear these on your hands.
2. **mayor** [mear] : the head of the government of a town or city.

4

however, that he later went to London, where he became one of the owners of a theatrical company called the Lord Chamberlain's [1] Men. It seems he was an actor before he began to write plays. He wrote thirty-eight plays, as well as poetry. After his death, some friends of Shakespeare collected his work and published it in 1623.

In 1599, Shakespeare's company built one of the most famous theatres in London, the Globe Theatre. The company changed its name to the King's Men in 1603, when James I became king, and from 1609 its main theatre was the Blackfriars.

Shakespeare became rich and successful and retired to Stratford-upon-Avon in 1613. He died there on 23 April 1616.

Visitors to Stratford-upon-Avon today can see many of the buildings associated with Shakespeare's life, including the house where he was born and Anne Hathaway's cottage. They can also visit the Royal Shakespeare Theatre and go to performances of Shakespeare's plays.

The modern reconstruction of the **Globe Theatre** in London,
very near the site of Shakespeare's Globe, which was destroyed by fire in 1613.

1.   **Lord Chamberlain** : a very important official at the royal court.

1 Comprehension check

Answer the questions.

1 Why do people like to think that Shakespeare was born on 23 April?

2 What kind of school did Shakespeare go to?

3 What are the 'missing years'?

4 Where did Shakespeare work when he went to London?

5 What did Shakespeare do before he started writing plays?

6 How many plays did Shakespeare write?

7 Who were the King's Men?

8 When and where did Shakespeare die?

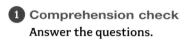 **INTERNET** PROJECT

Go to the Internet and go to www.blackcat-cideb.com or www.cideb.it .
Insert the title or part of the title of the book into our search engine.
Open the page to *Julius Caesar*. Click on the Internet project link.
Scroll down the page until you find the title of this book and click on
the relevant link for this project.

In pairs or small groups, plan a weekend in Stratford-upon-Avon, and then
present your plans to the class.

Download some
pictures of places
that interest you to
include in your
report.

Say:
▶ where you are
going to stay
▶ what historical
places you are
going to visit
▶ where you are
going to eat
▶ what other things
you are going to
do

The Historical *Julius Caesar*

Julius Caesar was born in Rome in 100 BCE[1]. His family was old and aristocratic, but not rich or influential. In 78, he became a legal prosecutor and went to Rhodes, an important Greek island in the Aegean sea, to study public speaking. On the way to Rhodes, Caesar was captured by pirates. He persuaded the pirates to ask for a lot of money to set him free, which made him seem more important to the Roman people. When he was free, he got some ships and soldiers and attacked the pirates and executed them.

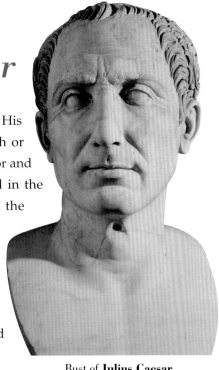

Bust of **Julius Caesar**
(1st century BCE).

His political career progressed, and in 61 he was made governor of Spain. In 60 he returned to Rome, and together with Crassus and Pompey he formed the first *triumvirate*, the three important men who ruled Rome.

In 60, Caesar was made governor of Gaul (modern France). During the next eight years, he conquered northern Gaul, which was not under Roman control. But back in Rome, Crassus died in 53 and in 52 the Senate made Pompey the only *consul*, the only leader.

In 49, the Senate ordered Caesar to give up his position. He did not obey, and on January 10-11 he crossed the Rubicon, a small river separating Gaul from Italy: this marked the beginning of civil war. Pompey left Rome and after only three months Caesar ruled all of Italy. He then took Spain and went after Pompey to Egypt where, in 48, Pompey was murdered by an Egyptian officer. Caesar stayed in Egypt for a while, and had a love affair with Queen Cleopatra.

1. **BCE** : abbreviation for Before the Common Era, used nowadays by many people instead of BC (Before Christ). CE (Common Era) is also often used instead of AD (Anno Domini). However, both systems refer to exactly the same periods of time.

In 48, Caesar took the title of *dictator*, and spent the next four years fighting opponents in Africa and Spain before returning to Rome. But a group of sixty senators, including Gaius Cassius and Marcus Junius Brutus, plotted to kill him. On 14 March 44, a date called the Ides of March by the Romans, Caesar entered the Senate House: he was stabbed twenty-three times. After his death, another thirteen years of civil war followed.

1 Comprehension check
Answer the following questions.

1   What did Caesar do when he was captured by pirates, and what does this tell us about his character?
2   Why did Caesar cross the Rubicon, and what happened as a result?
3   How did he die, and what happened after his death?

The Death of Julius Caesar (1798) by Vincenzo Camuccini.
Both the murdered Caesar and the assassins are presented as noble. Caesar is stabbed by many people, but this emphasises the collaboration among the assassins, not their brutality.

The Characters

JULIUS CAESAR

CALPURNIA
Caesar's wife

MARCUS ANTONIUS
*Triumvir after
the death of Caesar*

MARCUS BRUTUS
Conspirator

PORTIA
Brutus's wife

CASSIUS
Conspirator

OCTAVIUS CAESAR, M. EMILIUS LEPIDUS *Triumvirs after the death of Caesar*
CASCA, TREBONIUS, DECIUS BRUTUS, METELLUS CIMBER *Conspirators*
Friends and servants of Brutus and Cassius

PART ONE

CAESAR IN·ROME

For four years two Roman armies fought a terrible war against each other.  One army supported Pompey and his sons, and the other army supported Julius Caesar. At last the army of Julius Caesar was successful — he defeated his enemies. Then he decided to return to the city of Rome. His friends organised a magnificent procession through the city. They wanted to honour his victory.

The people of Rome had heard about Caesar's great victory, and they were excited. Many of them came out into the streets. This was their opportunity to see the great man.

Two of the Roman tribunes [1] were also out in the streets that day. They, too, had heard about Caesar's victory, but they were not happy. Flavius and Marullus thought that Caesar was too powerful. They thought he might use his power in a bad way. They knew that Caesar's friends wanted to make him king. They did not want a king. They wanted to protect the people of Rome from Caesar.

Flavius and Marullus walked among the happy crowd of people. Then Marullus stopped some of the citizens:

---

1. **tribunes** : officers elected by the people of Rome to protect their rights.

CAESAR IN ROME

'What are you doing?' he asked angrily. 'Why aren't you working today? It's not a holiday — you should be working!'

'I am here to see Caesar, sir,' one of the men replied. 'We all are. This is a great day for Rome, and we...'

Flavius interrupted the man.

'What kind of work do you do?'

'I make shoes, sir,' the man told him.

'You should be working, not walking around the city with all these other men!' Flavius told him. 'But why do you want to see Caesar?'

'We want to see the procession,' the man explained. 'Caesar has beaten[1] his enemies, and we want to see the victory procession. That's why we're here today.'

Now Marullus spoke to the man again. He was still angry.

'Why are you happy about Caesar's victory? You liked Pompey, too, didn't you? You cheered his victories once — and now you cheer the man who killed Pompey's sons!'

The shoemaker and his friends did not know what to say to Flavius and Marullus. Everything that the tribunes said was true. They had cheered Pompey's victories once. But Pompey was dead, and the great man of Rome was now Julius Caesar!

'Go home, my friends!' Flavius told the men. 'Go home, and remember your old hero Pompey.'

The men began to leave the centre of the city. They were ashamed of their behaviour. Flavius and Marullus watched them for a while.

Caesar's return to Rome occurred[2] at the same time as the feast of Lupercal.[3] This was a time when the whole city came together. There was a special race in honour of the Roman god Lupercus. Some of the most important young Romans took part in this race.

Caesar and his wife Calpurnia went to see the games. Many people walked with Caesar and his wife, because he was the most important man in Rome.

---

1. **beaten** : won a victory over (*to beat-beat-beaten*).
2. **occurred** : happened.
3. **feast of Lupercal** : ancient Roman Festival held each year in February. Each Lupercalia began with the sacrifice of goats and a dog.

Some of the people with Caesar were real friends, but some of them did not like him.

Caesar called out to one of the young men with him:

'Antony! Mark Antony!'

Mark Antony ran up to Caesar. He was dressed in the costume of an athlete.

'I am here, Caesar.'

The great man looked at his young friend, and then he looked at his wife, Calpurnia.

'Remember the old tradition,' he said, 'If a man who is running in this race stops for a moment to touch a woman, it will bring her luck. She will have

Julius Caesar

children. Remember that when you are running today. Stop for a moment, and touch Calpurnia.'

'I will remember, Caesar,' Mark Antony said. 'When Caesar commands, we all obey!'

At that moment a strange figure came out of the crowd around Caesar. It was an old man, and his clothes were dirty and poor. He was a soothsayer. [1] He stepped forward.

'Caesar!' he called.

Caesar looked around.

'Somebody called my name,' he said to the people round him. 'Who is it?'

The soothsayer approached the great man.

'I have a message for you,' he announced. The Ides of March [2] are dangerous for you, Caesar. Be careful of the Ides of March!'

Caesar turned to his friend Brutus.

'I didn't hear what he said, Brutus. What did he tell me?'

Brutus repeated the old man's message.

'He told you to be careful of the Ides of March.'

'He's an old fool,' Caesar commented. 'Let's go on — I want to see the race.'

Caesar moved forward, and most of the crowd of people followed him. Two men did not move forward, however. One of them was Brutus. The other man was called Cassius.

'Are you going to watch the race?' Cassius asked.

'I don't think so,' Brutus replied. 'You go, if you want.'

'I've been watching you recently,' Cassius said. 'We were close friends once. But nowadays you ignore your friends. We're not important to you. What's happened to you?'

'You're wrong, Cassius. If I have ignored my friends, I'm sorry. The truth is, I have been thinking a lot recently. I've been trying to make a very difficult decision. I'm sorry if I've offended you. But you can be sure that you're one of my best friends.'

Cassius smiled.

1. **soothsayer** : person who can predict the future.
2. **Ides of March** : 15 March.

'I'm glad to hear that, Brutus, because there's something I want to ask you. Many of the best people in Rome have been speaking about you. They want Rome to be free, they don't want to have Caesar...'

Both men heard a great shout from the crowd at the race.

'What was that?' cried Brutus. 'I hope the people haven't decided to make Caesar king!'

'You hope they haven't?' asked Cassius. 'Then you don't want him to be king?'

'No, Cassius, I don't want Caesar to be king. I am his good friend, and I love him — but I don't want him to be king.' He looked at Cassius for a moment, and thought deeply. 'I can see you want to tell me something important. What is it? Why did you want to talk to me?'

'You're right, Brutus,' Cassius said. 'I do have something important to tell you. It's about Caesar. He's just an ordinary man like you and me — why are we afraid of him? I remember once he challenged me [1] to swim across the Tiber [2] against him. It was winter, and the water was cold. We both went into the river, and began to swim. Suddenly Caesar cried out, "Help, Cassius, help!" I saved his life that day. And now they want to make him king! Another time we were both in Spain with the army. Caesar was ill, and he cried out to me, "Give me some water, Cassius — bring me some water!" And now they want to make him king!'

Brutus and Cassius heard another great shout.

'Perhaps they will make him king,' Brutus said. 'Perhaps they've already done it!'

'Why should Caesar be our king?' Cassius demanded angrily. 'What's so special about him?'

'I know now why you wanted to speak to me, and I can imagine what you want to do. I will think about what you have said, and we'll talk about this again. For now, remember one thing — I, too, love Rome, and I love freedom!'

Just then there was another great shout from the crowd.

'What's happening there?' Brutus said. 'Let's wait until the people come out, and then we can ask someone.'

1. **challenged me** : invited me to compete with him.
2. **Tiber** : the river which runs through Rome.

The text and **beyond**

PET **1** **Comprehension check**

Read Part One and the questions below. For each question, choose the correct answer — A, B, C or D.

1 Flavius and Marullus did not want to celebrate Caesar's victory because
   A ☐ they preferred Pompey.
   B ☐ they did not like being with the people of Rome.
   C ☐ they thought Caesar had too much power.
   D ☐ they wanted another man to be king of Rome.

2 The shoemaker felt ashamed because
   A ☐ he honoured his hero's enemy.
   B ☐ he still preferred Pompey to Caesar.
   C ☐ he did not know that Pompey was dead.
   D ☐ he thought Caesar was Pompey's friend.

3 Caesar wanted Mark Antony to touch Calpurnia because
   A ☐ it would bring Caesar good luck.
   B ☐ it would help her have a child.
   C ☐ it would help Mark Antony win the race.
   D ☐ Caesar liked old traditions.

4 The soothsayer told Caesar that the Ides of March would
   A ☐ bring him good luck.
   B ☐ be dangerous for him.
   C ☐ be dangerous for Rome.
   D ☐ be dangerous for Calpurnia.

5 Brutus did not pay much attention to his friends because he
   A ☐ no longer considered them important.
   B ☐ was worried about Caesar's great power.
   C ☐ was worried about the Ides of March.
   D ☐ was involved in plans to make Caesar king.

6 Cassius told about how he had saved Caesar to show that
   A ☐ he was a better swimmer than Caesar.
   B ☐ Caesar was afraid of him.
   C ☐ he was a real friend of Caesar's.
   D ☐ Caesar was not such a great man.

2 Vocabulary

Find the words from Part One that belong to the five categories in the word square. To help you, the words are already given below but with missing letters.

War   _ r _ _   _ n _ m _ _ _   v _ _ _ _ _ _   _ ea _ _ n

Government   _ _ _ g   c _ _ _ z _ _ s   _ r _ b _ _ _

Special events   f _ _ s _   _ _ l _ _ _ _   pr _ _ _ _ _ _ _ _

Sports   _ _ _ le _ _   _ ac _   ch _ _ _ _ _ _ _

Rome   _ i _ y   _ _ owd   _ _ re _ _ _

```
G  C  T  J  K  W  H  E  R  E  Y  E  S  T  E
O  S  R  W  T  C  H  A  L  L  E  N  G  E  D
V  O  B  O  L  R  G  N  A  T  H  J  H  M  P
I  O  A  R  W  H  I  S  T  R  E  E  T  S  R
C  R  C  R  B  D  F  B  T  P  E  O  P  K  O
T  A  I  H  M  O  E  R  U  S  E  S  A  N  C
O  C  T  A  D  Y  A  O  G  N  E  A  T  C  E
R  E  I  C  T  O  S  L  K  E  E  B  U  T  S
Y  T  Z  C  A  H  T  T  E  N  E  M  I  E  S
S  H  E  D  O  N  L  O  P  I  K  G  B  O  I
A  U  N  N  S  A  R  E  O  F  I  T  E  N  O
N  L  S  A  T  T  A  C  T  K  N  E  A  B  N
G  R  Y  C  I  T  Y  H  O  E  G  O  T  E  D
F  L  A  C  T  R  T  K  L  A  T  V  E  R  Y
Y  O  H  O  L  I  D  A  Y  T  H  E  N  H  E
```

3 Listening

Listen to two Roman citizens talking about Caesar and fill in the gaps.

Man : It's a good thing, I tell you! We need a (**1**) .... man in Rome. Caesar's the man we need. He's the (**2**) .... friend.

Woman : Why do you say he's the people's friend? What's he ever done for me, I want to know? I don't (**3**) .... him. I think he wants to be (**4**) ....

Man : King? Who told you Caesar wants to be king? Where did you (**5**) .... that?

Woman : Flavius said something about it.

Man : Those (6) .... — you don't want to listen to what they say! They're (7) .... of Caesar. They say a lot of (8) .... things about him — but they're frightened of him all the same.

Woman : You don't want a king in Rome, do you?

Man : Why not? A king's all (9) .... if he's a friend of the people. At least Caesar's a strong man — not like Flavius and that other one, Marullus!

4 The Lupercalia

Read the text about the Roman festival of Lupercalia, and fill in the gaps with the words in the box.

> sacrificed   cut   which   when
> who   then   began   ran

The Lupercalia was one of the oldest Roman religious festivals. It (1) ....
when the people of Rome lived mostly in the country, but it continued to be celebrated even (2) .... Rome was a great city.

It was held each year on 15 February at the Lupercal — the cave of the mythological founders of Rome, Romulus and Remus. The people (3) .... led the celebrations were called Luperci (in 44 BCE, Mark Antony was one of the Luperci). First, the Luperci (4) .... two goats and a dog. (5) .... the skin of the goats was (6) .... into long strips. Two of the Luperci, who were noble Romans, wore some of the strips, and held another one. They then (7) .... around the city and hit men to purify them, and women to make them fertile. In fact, the word 'February' comes from the Latin verb 'februare', (8) .... means 'to purify'.

T: GRADE 5

Speaking: festivals

Now present a short talk to the class about a festival in your country. Bring in some pictures or objects that show some aspects of this festival. Use the questions to help you.

1 What is the origin of this festival?

2 When is it held?

3 What are the ceremonies connected with it?

4 Is there any particular food associated with this festival?

5 What personal memories do you have of this festival?

Before you read

1 Listening

PET

Listen to the beginning of Part Two. For each question, put a tick (✓) in the correct box.

1 Mark Antony talked to Caesar about Cassius
   A ☐ before the race.
   B ☐ after the race.
   C ☐ during the race.

2 Mark Antony thinks that Cassius
   A ☐ will not hurt Caesar.
   B ☐ will hurt Caesar
   C ☐ will help Caesar.

3 The crowd shouted because
   A ☐ Caesar made a good speech.
   B ☐ Caesar took the crown.
   C ☐ Caesar didn't take the crown.

4 Caesar fell to the ground because
   A ☐ Casca pushed him.
   B ☐ he didn't feel well.
   C ☐ he didn't watch his step.

5 Cassius thinks that Brutus
   A ☐ shares his ideas about Caesar.
   B ☐ disagrees with him about Caesar.
   C ☐ needs to understand better who Caesar is.

6 Casca believes that the strange events in Rome mean that
   A ☐ the gods are not at all happy with Rome.
   B ☐ Rome is in great danger.
   C ☐ Caesar will soon become king.

PART TWO

THE CONSPIRACY

The race was finished, and people were leaving. Brutus and Cassius watched as Caesar approached them. There was still a crowd of people around the great man. They could see that Caesar was speaking to Mark Antony, but they could not hear what he was saying.

'Look at Cassius,' Caesar said to Antony. 'I don't trust men like him. He's a thin, hungry-looking man. He's always thinking, too — that type of man is dangerous.'

'You're wrong, Caesar,' Mark Antony replied. 'Cassius is a good Roman. You need not be afraid of him.'

'Afraid? Me! You don't understand me,' Caesar said. 'I am Caesar, and I don't fear anyone. I only meant that Cassius is a dangerous kind of man. He thinks and studies, and he has no pleasures in life. That sort of man hates greatness in others.'

Cassius whispered to Brutus, 'Look, there's Casca. We'll ask him what's been going on.' He touched Casca's arm as the crowd passed.

'What is it?' Casca asked. 'Why do you want me?'

'What happened back there?' asked Brutus. 'Why was everybody shouting?'

THE CONSPIRACY

'Antony offered Caesar a crown,' Casca told them. 'Caesar refused to take it, and then the people began to shout.'

'Why was there a second shout?' Brutus asked.

'The same thing,' Casca said. 'Antony offered the crown a second time, and Caesar refused it again. The crowd cheered[1] again.'

'They shouted three times,' Cassius said. 'Why did they shout the third time?'

'For the same reason,' Casca explained.

'Tell us everything that happened,' Brutus asked.

'It was stupid,' Casca told them. 'The whole thing was stupid. Antony offered Caesar the crown three times. Caesar refused to take it each time. The people applauded him each time he refused. I think he wanted to take it, but he couldn't. The people cheered him when he refused it, you see. They didn't want him to have it. Suddenly Caesar looked ill, and he fell to the ground. He couldn't speak.'

'Was that all?' Brutus and Cassius wanted to know.

'Yes,' said Casca, 'that was everything. When Caesar recovered, he came away — but he didn't look happy. That man wants to be king, in my opinion.'

The three men discussed the events of the day for a while, and agreed to meet again soon. Then they separated. When he was alone, Cassius thought about his conversation with Brutus.

'You are beginning to think like me, my friend,' Cassius thought. 'I can see that you don't want Caesar to be king. I am pleased about that, very pleased.'

That night there was a terrible storm in Rome. People were afraid, and there were reports of very strange events. Some people said they had seen flames fall out of the sky onto the city. Other people said they had seen a lion walking in the streets.

Casca was walking in the city during the storm. He, too, had seen strange things, and he was afraid. He believed the gods were angry with Rome. Suddenly he met Cassius and began to talk about the things he had seen.

'You're a fool, my friend,' Cassius told him. 'The gods are not angry with Rome. These events mean something else. The gods are telling us about a

---

1. **cheered** : shouted to show that they agreed and that they thought he was a good person.

Julius Caesar

great danger facing the city. [1] You say you saw a lion in the streets... there is a man in Rome who reminds me of a lion, Casca — a lion who is dangerous to the city.'

'You mean Caesar, don't you?' Casca said. 'I've heard that the Senate is going to offer him the crown once more tomorrow.'

'I have a knife,' said Cassius. 'I will kill myself with it if I must, but I will never live under tyranny.' [2]

'I'm the same,' Casca agreed. 'I will die if I have to, but I will die a free man.'

'We don't have to die, my friend,' Cassius said slowly. 'We are not dangerous. It is the lion that...'

The two men looked at each other for a long moment.

'... must die,' said Casca slowly. 'I agree with you. The lion must die.'

Casca and Cassius shook hands.

'We are not the only ones,' Cassius said. 'There are other men who think like us in Rome.'

Cassius introduced Casca to the other conspirators. They talked together, and everybody agreed about one thing. They wanted Brutus to join the conspiracy. They all knew the story of Brutus's ancestors, who had driven [3] the Tarquin [4] kings from the city. They all knew that Brutus was popular with the people. The people respected him. With Brutus on their side, the conspiracy could succeed.

'He will join us, I'm sure of it,' Cassius told the conspirators. 'I have spoken to him, and I know he wants to join. I have sent him some anonymous letters. I think they will persuade him. Brutus is a man who needs to be persuaded before he acts.'

While the conspirators were meeting in the centre of the city, Brutus was walking in his garden. He was thinking about Caesar and the problems of Rome. Caesar was his friend, but he was sure that Caesar would be a bad king.

---

1. **about a great danger facing the city** : that something terrible will happen in the city.
2. **tyranny** : a government in which a person or a small group of people have power over everyone else.
3. **driven** : forced (*to drive - drove - driven*).
4. **Tarquin** : family of Roman kings.

THE CONSPIRACY

'He must die,' Brutus thought sadly. 'He is not dangerous now, but he will be dangerous if he becomes king — therefore he must die.' Brutus was not happy with his thoughts.

The servant-boy, Lucius, came into the garden. He was carrying a letter.

'Excuse me, sir,' he said. 'I found this letter in the house. I don't know who brought it to the house. Perhaps someone threw it through the window.'

Brutus took the letter, and began to read it.

> WAKE UP, BRUTUS! SPEAK! DO SOMETHING! JUSTICE!
>   A FRIEND.

Brutus had received many letters like this one in the past few days. Now he was convinced that Rome needed him — his mind was made up![1]

Brutus heard a knock at the door of the house, and then men's voices.

'Who is it, Lucius?' he called out.

'It's Cassius, sir,' the boy replied.

'Is he alone?'

'No, sir, there are other men with him. I don't know who they are, because their faces are covered.'

'The conspirators!' thought Brutus. He was frightened for a moment, but then he came forward to meet the men.

Brutus welcomed the conspirators to his house, and they all shook hands. Everyone wanted Brutus to be their leader — they admired and respected him. Soon they were all discussing their plans for the assassination.

Cassius made several important suggestions to the conspirators:

'We should all make an oath [2] to be loyal to each other,' he said. 'Our oath should be a solemn one.'

'No,' said Brutus, 'we don't need to make any oaths to the gods. We're all Romans, and men of honour. That's sufficient, in my view.'

'We agree with Brutus,' the other conspirators said. 'When a Roman says he will do something, there is no need of oaths.'

---

1. **his mind was made up** : he had decided.
2. **oath** : solemn promise.

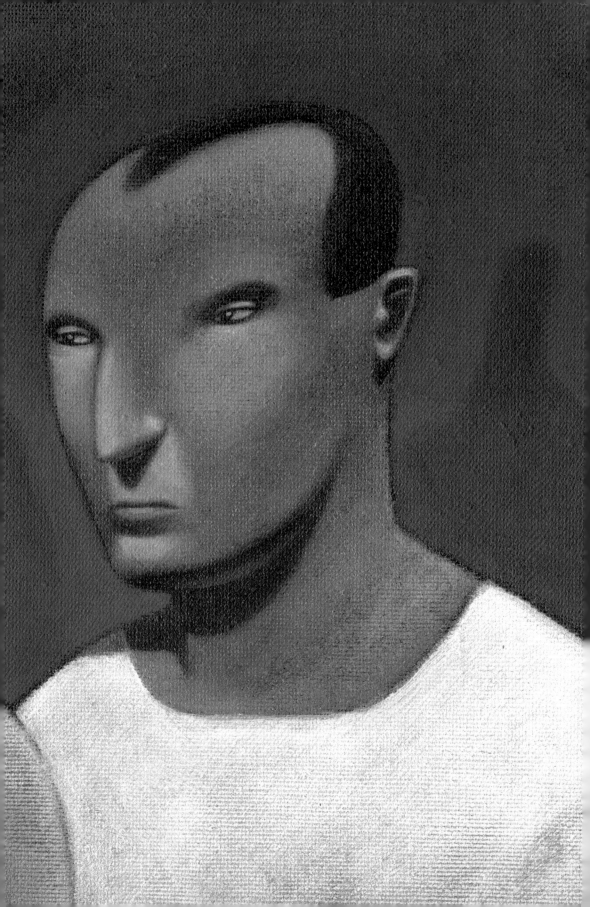

Julius Caesar

'There's another thing,' Cassius told them. 'The people of Rome will be angry and frightened when they know that Caesar is dead. I think we should ask Cicero [1] to join us — he can explain our actions to the people. Everybody will listen to him, and he is the best speaker in Rome. Why don't we ask him to be one of us?'

'It's a good idea,' said Casca, 'the people will listen to what Cicero says.'

'No!' said Brutus once again. 'Cicero is an old man, and he will never follow us. Let's not think of him any more.'

'Very well,' Cassius agreed. 'We'll manage without Cicero. Then there is the question of Mark Antony — what shall we do with him? He loves Caesar, and he is clever and powerful. We should kill him as well. He's dangerous!'

Brutus disagreed with Cassius for the third time.

'Antony is nothing once Caesar is dead,' he argued. 'There's no need to kill him — he won't be able to do anything to us. I say there is no reason to kill Antony. Besides,[2] if we kill Antony as well as Caesar, what will we say to the people of Rome? They will think we are just murderers!'

'But still,' Cassius went on, 'Antony loves Caesar. He's a dangerous —'

'Brutus is right,' one of the conspirators interrupted Cassius. 'Antony can do nothing to us after Caesar is dead. Let him live!'

'Then we agree,' Cassius announced. 'We'll kill Caesar this morning when he arrives at the Senate House. [3] We will all go to his house this morning, and walk with him to the Senate House.'

---

1. **Cicero** : a famous speaker and politician (106-43 BCE). He did not support Caesar.
2. **Besides** : Also.
3. **Senate House** : place where the senators met in ancient Rome. The most permanent governing council in Ancient Rome.

The text and **beyond**

1 Comprehension check
Answer the questions

1 What strange signs did the people see during the storm?

2 What, according to Cassius, did the lion represent?

3 Why did Cassius show Casca his knife?

4 Why did the conspirators want Brutus to join them?

5 What was Brutus's relationship with Caesar?

6 How did Cassius convince Brutus that Rome needed him?

7 Why didn't Brutus want Mark Antony to be killed?

2 Characters
Who said what and why? Match the quotes with the character who said them, and then match the quotes with the reasons why they said them. You can use some characters more than once.

WHO

Casca (Cc)   Julius Caesar (JC)

Cassius (Cs)   Brutus (B)

1 ☐ ☐ 'It was stupid.'

2 ☐ ☐ 'He loves Caesar.'

3 ☐ ☐ 'They didn't want him to have it.'

4 ☐ ☐ 'The gods are not angry with Rome.'

5 ☐ ☐ 'They will think we are just murderers!'

6 ☐ ☐ 'He thinks and studies, and he has no pleasures in life.'

7 ☐ ☐ 'The lion must die.'

8 ☐ ☐ 'Brutus is a man who needs to be persuaded before he acts.'

A He is saying why the conspirators should also kill Mark Antony.

B He is trying to show that the real danger to Rome is Caesar.

C He is explaining why he sent anonymous letters.

D He is joining the conspiracy against Caesar.

E He is saying what he thinks of Antony offering and Caesar refusing the crown.

F He is saying why the crowd cheered Caesar.

G He is explaining why they shouldn't kill Mark Antony.

H He is saying why he does not trust Cassius.

3 **Chickens, livers and lightning: telling the future in ancient Rome**

Read the short article about soothsayers in Ancient Rome, and then discuss the questions with your partner. Report your ideas to the class.

The Romans, like most ancient peoples, believed that the gods showed people the future. They did this with certain signs that certain specialised people could read. These specialised people, or soothsayers, were called *haruspices* and *augurs*. Haruspices read the internal organs of animals like the heart, liver and lungs. Haruspices were not generally Romans, they came from another part of ancient Italy called Etruria.

The augurs understood what the gods wanted by interpreting thunder and lightning. They also watched how birds flew in the sky. Another interesting technique involved chickens. Chickens were kept in a cage. The cage was opened and the chickens were given food. The augur watched closely the chickens: Did they make noise? Did they run away? Did they eat a lot? A little? These augurs were often consulted by generals before important military battles. However, by the time of Julius Caesar, many educated Roman did not believe in augurs or haruspices.

1   What are some of the signs that are mentioned in Part Two?

2   How are they interpreted?

3   Do people in your country try to 'see the future'? What techniques do they use?

4   What do you think about modern soothsayers?

4 **Summary**

Number the paragraphs in the right order to make a summary of Parts One-Two. The first one has been done for you.

A ☐   There was also a race being held in honour of the god Lupercus. Caesar too went to see the races.

B ☐   Afterwards Mark Antony offered Caesar a crown three times. Each time Caesar refused and the crowd cheered.

C ☐   He told Caesar to be careful of the Ides of March. Caesar did not take him seriously and went to see the races.

D ☐   Brutus was finally convinced. He and the other conspirators decided to kill Caesar in the Senate.

E ☐1   Caesar returned victorious to Rome after four years of war against Pompey. The common people came out to see the new great man of Rome.

F ☐   However, many Romans thought that Caesar really wanted to become king. One of them was Cassius. He began to plan a conspiracy.

G ☐   Cassius wanted Brutus to help him. But he knew that Brutus had to be persuaded.

H ☐ He began to send Brutus anonymous letters. They asked Brutus to defend Rome against Caesar.

I ☐ As he was walking there, a strange man stopped him. This man was a soothsayer.

🎧 Listening activity: the questions can be found online at www.blackcat-cideb.com. Go to the *Julius Caesar* page.

Before you read

🎧 **1** Listening

PET

You will hear a conversation between Brutus and his wife Portia. For each question, put a tick (✓) in the correct box.

1 Brutus could not sleep because he was thinking about
   A ☐ his wife.
   B ☐ the conspiracy to kill Caesar.
   C ☐ the terrible storm in Rome.

2 Portia could not sleep because she was thinking about
   A ☐ her husband and his troubles.
   B ☐ Caesar refusing the crown.
   C ☐ the terrible storm in Rome.

3 Brutus told Portia that he was not sleeping because
   A ☐ he had to make an important decision.
   B ☐ he was afraid.
   C ☐ he was feeling ill.

4 What was unusual about the men who came to Portia and Brutus's house?
   A ☐ She could not see their faces.
   B ☐ She did not recognise their faces.
   C ☐ They had angry expressions on their faces.

5 Portia thought Brutus did not tell her the truth because
   A ☐ he was afraid.
   B ☐ she was not a man.
   C ☐ she always told his secrets to her friends.

6 Brutus decided to tell Portia the truth because he realised that she was
   A ☐ really worried.
   B ☐ brave.
   C ☐ intelligent enough to help him.

PART THREE

HUSBANDS AND WIVES

Their plan was ready, and the conspirators left Brutus. It was now almost morning, and Brutus could not sleep. He walked up and down in the garden. He was thinking about the assassination. Suddenly he heard a noise, and there was someone standing in front of him. It was his wife.

'Portia! Why are you here? It's still very early, you should be sleeping.'

'I couldn't sleep, Brutus. I was thinking about you. You've been strange in the last few days. I know you are worried about something. Tell me what it is — perhaps I can help you.'

'It's nothing, Portia,' Brutus told her. 'I have not been well, that's all. Go back to bed, please.'

'Brutus! We are husband and wife — we shouldn't have secrets from each other. I want to know the truth. Who were those men that came to the house? Why were their faces covered? Tell me what is going on!'

Brutus said nothing for a moment.

'Do you think that I cannot keep secrets because I am a woman?' Portia asked him. 'Are you afraid to trust me? Is that why you don't say anything? I'm not like other women, Brutus. I am strong, and I am brave. I have done something to prove my courage to you. Look!'

Julius Caesar

As Portia spoke, she pulled her gown [1] to one side. There was a terrible wound [2] on her leg!

'I did that with a knife,' she told her husband proudly. 'I did it to prove that I am brave enough to know your secrets.'

Brutus looked at the wound on his wife's leg, and he remembered his love for Portia.

'I will tell you everything,' he said. 'You are a courageous woman, and you deserve to know your husband's secrets.' He told her everything — why he thought Caesar was dangerous, and about the plan to kill him.

Caesar did not rest well that night. He was kept awake by the storm, and his wife slept badly. He was worried, and he told his servant to prepare a sacrifice to the gods.

His wife, Calpurnia, did not want him to go to the Senate House. She asked him to stay at home.

'I'm frightened,' she told him. 'The gods are angry today, and I hear strange things have happened in the city. There was a lion in the streets, and people heard the sounds of battle. No one knows what it means, but I am frightened. Please don't go.'

At first Caesar ignored his wife's fears. He told her that he was not afraid, and that he had to go to the Senate House. Then his servant came in.

'We have done what you told us,' the man said. 'We have sacrificed an animal to the gods.'

'Well?' asked Caesar. 'What happened at the sacrifice?'

'It was very strange, sir,' the servant said. 'When the animal was dead, we looked inside the body — but we could not find its heart!'

'It's a sign from the gods!' cried Calpurnia. 'It means that there is danger for you today. Stay at home, Caesar, stay at home.'

'All right, Calpurnia,' Caesar agreed. 'I will stay at home today. I will ask Antony to say that I am not well today.'

Decius, one of the conspirators, came to Caesar's house. He smiled, and greeted the great man warmly.

---

1. **gown** : robe, long dress.
2. **wound** [wu:nd]: cut made with a knife.

'Good morning, Caesar. I will walk with you to the Senate House this morning.'

'Good morning, Decius,' Caesar replied. 'Please take a message to the senators for me — I am not going to the Senate today.'

'Not going!' Decius cried. 'Why not, Caesar? What shall I tell the senators? They're all expecting you today.'

Caesar said, 'An animal I had sacrificed had no heart. That is all they need to know. But there is another reason, Decius. I can tell you because you are a friend. Calpurnia asked me not to go. She dreamt last night that the people of Rome washed their hands in my blood. The dream frightened her. She thinks it means danger for me, and she does not want me to go.'

Decius thought quickly. He knew that he had to persuade Caesar to come to the Senate House that morning.

'I can tell you the meaning of that dream, Caesar!' Decius said suddenly. 'It does not mean danger for you. You are the life-blood of the city of Rome. The people wash their hands in your blood, and they become pure and strong.'

Caesar was pleased at this interpretation of his wife's dream. It made him feel important.

'Do you think the dream really means that?' he asked Decius.

'Of course it does,' Decius replied. 'The Senate have decided to offer you the crown of Rome today — you will be king! Your blood will give strength to Rome. That's the meaning of Calpurnia's dream!'

'You're right, Decius,' Caesar decided. 'You have explained Calpurnia's dream correctly. I will go to the Senate this morning, after all.'

Now the rest of the conspirators arrived at Caesar's house. They were led by Brutus. Everybody greeted Caesar with smiles.

Then Antony arrived.

'You as well, Antony? I'm happy to see you here.'

Caesar was pleased to see his friends around him, and in a few minutes he was ready to leave.

'Your dream seems foolish now, Calpurnia,' he told his wife. 'I should not have listened to you.'

Then he left the house, talking and laughing with the conspirators.

The text and **beyond**

1 Comprehension check

Match the phrases in column A with those in column B to make complete sentences. There are four phrases in column B that you do not need to use.

A

1 ☐ Portia was curious about the men who came to her house
2 ☐ Portia wanted to know Brutus's secret
3 ☐ Portia cut her leg
4 ☐ Caesar could not sleep
5 ☐ Caesar decided not to go to the Senate House
6 ☐ Calpurnia was frightened by her dream
7 ☐ Decius gave a different interpretation of Calpurnia's dream
8 ☐ Caesar preferred Decius's interpretation of Calpurnia's dream

B

A because a sacrificed animal had no heart and Portia had a bad dream.
B because he had a terrible dream.
C because he was one of the conspirators.
D because it showed that he was a great man.
E because he thought Decius was more intelligent.
F because in it people washed their hands with Caesar's blood.
G because there was a terrible storm.
H because they wore masks.
I because she wanted to help him.
J because she wanted to show Brutus that she is brave.
K because she was a curious woman.
L because she heard them talk about a conspiracy.

2 Writing

Pretend that you are Calpurnia. Write in your diary, in about 150 words, your fears for your husband. Include the following information:

• what the soothsayer said
• what happened after the race
• what you dreamt
• what the results of the sacrifice were
• how Decius convinced your husband

3 Sentence transformation

Here are some sentences from Part Two. For each question, complete the second sentence so that it means the same as the first, using no more than three words. There's an example at the beginning (0).

0 Brutus said nothing for a moment.
Brutus did ....*not say anything*........... for a moment.

1 You've been strange in the last few days.
You've acted .... in the last few days.

2 I am not like other women.
Other women are .... from me.

3 At first Caesar ignored his wife's fears.
At first Caesar did not .... to his wife's fears.

4 Stay at home, Caesar.
Don't .... home, Caesar.

5 That is all they need to know.
They don't need to know .... else.

6 I can tell you the meaning of that dream.
I know .... that dream means.

> Brutus! We are husband and wife – we shouldn't have secrets from each other.

In the sentence above Portia means that it is not right for husbands and wives to have secrets from each other.
'Your dream seems foolish now, Calpurnia,' he told his wife. 'I should not have listened to you.'
Here Caesar means that it was not correct to listen to what Calpurnia told him.
Should or Shouldn't are used to indicate that the speaker believes that it is good or correct, or bad or wrong, to do something.
You shouldn't believe soothsayers. They don't really see the future.
You should trust Portia. She is very brave.

4 Should/shouldn't

Complete the sentences below with *should* or *shouldn't*. Use the words and phrases in the box.

stay   believe   trust   go to   kill (x2)

1 Flavius told the shoemaker that .... the procession in Caesar's honour.

2 Caesar thinks that Mark Antony .... men who think too much.

3 Cassius thinks that the conspirators .... Caesar.

4 Brutus thinks that the conspirators .... Mark Antony.

5 After hearing about the sacrifice, Calpurnia thinks that Caesar .... at home.

6 Decius thinks that Caesar .... Calpurnia's interpretation of the dream.

5 Word game
Complete the crossword puzzle.

Across

2 Show your approval or appreciation by clapping your hands.
4 The adjective from 'religion'.
7 Plot or a secret plan to do something bad or illegal.
10 A fight between two armies.
11 Visions that you see when you are sleeping.
12 Go near something or someone.
13 Silly or stupid.
15 Some, a number of.
16 Very bad weather with wind and rain.

Down

1 Not safe.
3 Amusements and enjoyable things.
5 A cut or other injury to the body.
6 Brutus's wife.
8 Brave.
9 To kill an animal for religious reasons.
14 Organ that pumps the blood.

Listening activity: the questions can be found online at www.blackcat-cideb.com. Go to the *Julius Caesar* page.

The Theatre
in Shakespeare's Times

Shakespeare went to London at an exciting time in the history of the theatre. In the recent past, plays had been performed by groups of 'travelling players'. The life of these travelling players was hard. They moved from town to town, usually performing in the courtyards of inns [1]. Theatre companies and actors were unpopular with the civil and church authorities: they were not seen as respectable people. Audiences at their performances did not behave with much respect, either.

1   **courtyards of inns** : inns were places to eat, drink and stay the night, and
    courtyards were the spaces in front of them or behind them.

Kermesse at Audenarde by the Dutch artist David Vinckboons (about 1576-1632).
The 'kermesse' was the annual fair held at Oudenaarde in Belgium (called Audenarde in French).
To the right of the centre you can see actors performing on a temporary stage.
The audience is not watching in respectful silence!

Few new plays were written for these groups of actors, and they mostly used traditional plays.

Even in Shakespeare's day the authorities in London did not have a very high opinion of the theatre and actors. But there were some professional theatre companies that were sponsored by important people. Shakespeare joined one of these companies, the Lord Chamberlain's Men (see page 5).

Building theatres for the professional companies was a new activity. It is not surprising that the first theatres looked a little like the old courtyards where so many actors had performed for years.

A **map of London** (1598) in Shakespeare's time.
The theatres were in Southwark, on the south bank of the River Thames.
There was only one bridge over the Thames, called London bridge.

One of the problems that the new theatres had in London was the health risk caused by large numbers of people being so close together in the audience, and in times of plague [1] the theatres were closed. There was also a risk of fire (as happened to the Globe in 1613) because all the buildings were made of wood. Because there was no artificial lighting, plays in Shakespeare's day were usually performed in the middle of the afternoon. Women were not allowed to act on stage, so female parts were played by boys. Costumes worn by the players could be very luxurious, and cost a lot of money, but they were always 16th-century

1 **plague** : a general name given for diseases that passed easily from person to person, and which usually killed. About 50 years after Shakespeare, the Great Plague of 1665 killed at least 70,000 people in London.

The **Globe Theatre** before it burnt down in 1613.
The flag, which could be seen from far away, was a sign that there was going to be a play that afternoon. A white flag meant there was going to be a comedy, a black flag meant a tragedy and a red flag meant a history play.

clothes: there was no attempt to create a historical feeling, so Shakespeare's Julius Caesar did not wear a toga. There was much less scenery [1] than in the theatre today: Shakespeare used his words to create a sense of place – but some stage machinery was used to make special sound effects, and to make some characters such as witches or spirits 'fly' over the stage. Special effects such as the noise of thunder could be made, too, but some spectacular effects were dangerous: a canon which exploded during a performance of Henry VIII caused the fire which burnt down the Globe.

1   **scenery** : objects and painting on stage which show where a play takes place.

1 Comprehension check
Answer the following questions.

1   What was the attitude to actors in Shakespeare's time?
2   What did early theatres look like?
3   What two big problems did early theatres face?
4   When were plays in Shakespeare's time usually performed? Why?
5   Who played female parts?
6   What can you say about costumes, scenery and special effects?

 INTERNET PROJECT

Go to the Internet and go to www.blackcat-cideb.com or www.cideb.it.
Insert the title or part of the title of the book into our search engine.
Open the page to *Julius Caesar*. Click on the Internet project link. Scroll down the page until you find the title of this book and click on the relevant link for this project.

▶ Find out about the building of the new Globe: whose idea was it, and what happened to him?
▶ Go on a virtual tour.
   Tell the class what you found interesting.

Before you read

ⓔ ① Listening

You will hear about the assassination of Caesar. For each question, put a tick (✓) in the correct box.

1 The soothsayer told Caesar that

    A ☐ it was the Ides of March.

    B ☐ Caesar was safe.

    C ☐ he should go inside the Senate House.

2 Artemidorus gave Caesar

    A ☐ a crown.

    B ☐ a letter.

    C ☐ a present.

3 Metellus Cimber asked Caesar

    A ☐ when his brother could return to Rome.

    B ☐ when his brother could leave Rome.

    C ☐ why his brother couldn't leave Rome.

4 Which conspirator first pulled out his knife?

    A ☐ Cassius

    B ☐ Brutus

    C ☐ Casca

5 Who was the last man Caesar saw just before he died?

    A ☐ Brutus

    B ☐ Casca

    C ☐ Cassius

6 After the assassination, the conspirators went to the centre of Rome to

    A ☐ escape the angry senators.

    B ☐ tell the people why they had killed Caesar.

    C ☐ hide Caesar's body from the people.

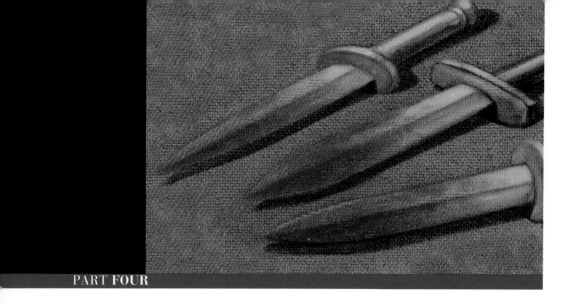

PART FOUR

THE ASSASSINATION

Caesar walked to the Senate House with the conspirators. As usual there was a crowd of people around the Senate. Caesar looked at them, and recognised the old soothsayer. He remembered the soothsayer's prediction about the Ides of March. He laughed, and summoned [1] the man to him.

'The Ides of March have come,' he said.

'True, Caesar,' the old man agreed. 'The Ides of March have come — but they have not gone yet!'

Another man in the crowd had a letter for Caesar. Artemidorus was a scholar. [2] He had heard about the conspiracy, and wanted to warn Caesar.

'Caesar, Caesar!' he cried. 'This letter is for you. It's important. Please read it.'

'Give me the letter,' Caesar commanded. 'I will read it later.'

'No, Caesar, read it now — read it now!' Artemidorus said.

Caesar was angry. Who did this man think he was? No one told Caesar what to do! He pushed the man away.

---

1. **summoned** : ordered to come.
2. **scholar** : a person who studies an academic subject and knows a lot about it.

THE ASSASSINATION

Caesar and the conspirators now entered the Senate House together. Caesar walked to his seat. When he was ready, he called out, 'I am ready to listen now. Who wants to ask the advice of Caesar and the Senate?'

The conspirators moved forward. They stood around Caesar's chair. One of them, Metellus Cimber, began to speak:

'Great Caesar,' he began, 'My brother is in exile. [1] When can he come back to the city?'

Now the other conspirators repeated Metellus Cimber's request.

'I also ask for the return of Publius Cimber,' Brutus said.

'So do I,' added Cassius.

'We all ask it!' the conspirators cried.

'I banished [2] Publius Cimber,' Caesar told them. 'I never change my mind, you know that. I will not change my mind now. Publius Cimber stays in exile.'

'Now!' Casca shouted. He took out his knife, and stabbed [3] Caesar.

Caesar cried out in pain and astonishment. He put his hand up to the wound. For a moment he did not understand what was happening. Then he looked around him, and he saw the conspirators approach him. Each man carried a knife in his hand.

Caesar was frightened for an instant. His eyes opened wide. Then he remembered that he was Julius Caesar, and his fear left him.

'Look at them!' he thought angrily. 'There's Casca, who's always hated me. And Cassius, who was my friend years ago. Am I going to die because of men like that?'

The conspirators lifted their knives in the air, and stabbed their enemy many times. Caesar tried to defend himself, but the conspirators were all around him. He could not get away from the sharp knives. Again and again he felt the blows [4] on his body, and soon he was weak.

'Calpurnia's dream was right, after all!' he thought.

Suddenly he felt very tired. He looked down, and he saw where his blood ran on the floor of the Senate House.

---

1. **in exile** : not allowed to live in Rome.
2. **banished** : sent away from Rome.
3. **stabbed** : hit with a knife.
4. **blows** : stabs with the knife.

He began to fall forward. He fell against one of the conspirators. Caesar looked up into the face of the man with the knife. He saw that it was Brutus, his friend.

'Even you, Brutus?' he asked.

Brutus stabbed him, and he fell dead.

The assassination was very quick. Caesar was attacked before the senators realised what was happening. When they saw the great man fall,

they were afraid. People ran from the Senate House in fear and confusion. Antony also left the building.

All the conspirators were covered in Caesar's blood. Their hands and clothes were red.

'We've done it!' Cassius cried excitedly. 'We've killed Caesar — Rome is free once more!'

Brutus looked at Cassius. Caesar had been his friend, and he was feeling sad.

Julius Caesar

'Think, my friends,' he said now. 'This is a great moment in history. In the future, when we are all dead, actors will play the death of Caesar in front of audiences. No one will ever forget what we have done today!'

For a while the conspirators talked among themselves, and then Brutus made a decision.

'We'll go into the centre of the city!' Brutus shouted. 'We'll tell the people of Rome what we have done. We'll explain why we have done it.'

The conspirators were still talking when Antony's servant came into the Senate House. He brought Brutus a message.

'My master greets you,' the servant said. 'He wants to know why you have killed Caesar. He says that he will follow you if you can give him good reasons.'

'Tell him to return to the Senate House,' Brutus told the messenger. 'I will explain everything to him. I promise Antony will be safe.'

'I'll tell him to come,' the servant said.

Antony returned to the Senate House a little while later. He had been a good friend of Caesar's, and he was very sad and angry at the murder. He stood over the body of his friend in silence for a while. Then he spoke to Brutus: 'Caesar is dead, and he was my friend. I don't know why you killed him — but I, too, am ready to die here. If you want to kill me as well, do it now.'

'We won't kill you,' Brutus said. 'You're in no danger from us. I'll tell you why we killed Caesar. When you know our reasons, you'll be our friend, too, I'm sure of it.'

'You are an honest man, Brutus,' Antony said. 'I'll listen to what you tell me.'

He shook Brutus by the hand. Then he shook the hand of each conspirator.

'I'm certain you had reasons for this,' he told them. 'But remember that I was Caesar's friend, and let me take his body to the city centre. I want to speak at his funeral.'

'Of course you can speak at his funeral,' Brutus promised.

Cassius did not want Antony to speak at the funeral. He knew that Antony was popular with the people, and he knew that he was a good speaker.

Antony might speak against the conspirators. Cassius tried to persuade Brutus to change his mind.

'Don't let Antony speak at the funeral,' he warned.

'There is nothing to fear,' Brutus told him. 'I will speak at the funeral first. I'll tell the people of Rome why we killed Caesar — I'll give them the reasons. Then Antony will speak as Caesar's friend. Let's go and prepare the funeral — we have a lot to do.'

Brutus and the conspirators left the Senate House. Antony was alone with the body of his friend.

'Forgive me, Caesar,' Antony whispered. [1] 'I spoke words of friendship with these men — but I lied to them. They have killed Caesar's body — but Caesar's spirit [2] will have revenge, I promise you!'

The funeral of Caesar took place in the centre of the city. The people of Rome stopped their work when they knew the great man was dead. They came to the funeral.

'We want to know why you killed Caesar!' they shouted at Brutus. 'Tell us why you did it!'

Brutus began to speak.

'Romans!' he cried. 'Listen to me, and I will tell you everything. Caesar was my friend, and I loved him. But I love Rome more than I loved Caesar. I killed Caesar because he wanted to be king. I killed him to defend the freedom of Rome.'

He paused for a moment.

The people talked among themselves. They had listened carefully to Brutus's speech, and they liked him. They believed what he said. They began to shout.

'Brutus will be our leader! We want Brutus for king!'

'Antony is coming here to speak to you,' Brutus went on. 'He was Caesar's friend, and he wants to speak at the funeral. He speaks with my permission. Listen to what he says, my friends.'

Antony began to speak.

---

1. **whispered** : spoke in a very low voice.
2. **spirit** : some people think that this part of a person continues to live when the body is dead.

Julius Caesar

'Friends, Romans,' he said, 'Brutus has told you that Caesar was ambitious, and Brutus is an honourable man. Was he ambitious when he made Rome rich from his victories? But was Caesar ambitious when he refused to be king at the feast of Lupercal? He refused three times, do you remember? Was that ambitious?'

The people spoke among themselves again.

'He refused the crown, that's right!' one of them said. 'I was there — I saw him. He refused it three times. He didn't want to be king!'

'Brutus is an honourable man,' Antony went on. 'I don't want to argue with him. I can only say this. Caesar loved the people of Rome. I've got his will [1] here. If you only knew how much he loved you!'

The people were very excited now. They wanted to hear Caesar's will.

'Read the will!' they cried. 'We want to hear the will! Read Caesar's will!'

'I cannot read the will,' Antony told them. 'You will be angry with Brutus and the other honourable men who killed Caesar.'

'Read it!' the people cried.

'Honourable men!' someone in the crowd shouted, 'I call them murderers.'

Antony began to read the document.

'Caesar left a piece of money to every Roman citizen. All his land and gardens here in Rome, he left to you, the people of Rome. Caesar was a great man, and he loved you all.'

'It's true,' the people cried, 'Caesar was a great man! Brutus and the others are traitors [2] and murderers!'

The crowd was angry now. Antony's speech had turned them against Brutus and the conspirators.

'Where are the traitors?' they shouted. 'We'll kill them — we'll kill them all!'

Brutus and the other conspirators ran away from the city.

1. **will** : legal document that gives instructions about what should happen to your money or possessions after you die.
2. **traitors** : enemies of their own country.

The text and **beyond**

1 Comprehension check
Answer these questions.

1 Why did Caesar laugh at the soothsayer?
2 Why didn't Caesar read Artemidorus's letter?
3 What excuse did the conspirators use to approach Caesar?
4 What was Caesar's reaction when he saw that Brutus was one of the conspirators?
5 Brutus said that the assassination would be remembered in the future. How?
6 How did Brutus feel after the assassination?
7 How did Mark Antony react to Caesar's death?
8 Why didn't Cassius want Antony to speak at Caesar's funeral?
9 What did Antony promise Caesar?
10 How did Brutus defend the assassination of Caesar before the Roman people?
11 How did the Roman people react to Brutus?
12 How did Antony show that Caesar was not ambitious?
13 According to Antony, what kind of man is Brutus?
14 How did Antony show that Caesar loved the Roman people?
15 How did the Roman people react to his speech?
16 What did the conspirators do after the speech?

T: GRADE 5

2 Speaking: entertainment
The incredible violence of the Roman shows with wild animals and battles between gladiators ended a long time ago. However, film directors continue to make successful films with gladiators and the other Roman games. Two of the most famous and successful films are *Spartacus* (1960) and *Gladiator* (2000)
Use the questions below to help you make a short presentation about violence in films.

1 Have you ever seen a film with gladiators?
2 Why do think people like films about gladiators? For the same reasons that the Romans liked to see real gladiators fight and die?
3 Do you watch films with lots of violence? Why or why not?
4 Do you think there should be less violence in films? Why or why not?
5 Are there any popular sports that are very dangerous? Which ones?
6 Do people watch these sports because they are dangerous?

INTERNET PROJECT

Go to the Internet and go to www.blackcat-cideb.com or www.cideb.it.
Insert the title or part of the title of the book into our search engine.
Open the page to *Julius Caesar*. Click on the Internet project link.
Scroll down the page until you find the title of this book and click on
the relevant link for this project.

**Answer the questions about
the 1960 film *Spartacus* and
the 2000 film *Gladiator*.**

1 Who were the directors
   of the two films?
2 Did these films win any
   awards? Which ones?
3 Who were the actors in
   them?
4 What is the historical event that inspired *Spartacus*?
5 When are the events in *Gladiator* supposed to take place?
6 In which of these two films is Julius Caesar a character?
7 Download a picture of the film you think looks more interesting and show it to the
   class.

 3 Fill in the gaps

Suetonius (about 69 CE - about 130 CE) was a Roman historian. His most famous
book was the *Lives of the Caesars*. Even though he lived after Julius Caesar,
historians think that he had access to much official information about the Roman
government.
Read the text below in which Suetonius describes how Caesar won the favour of
the people of Rome and his soldiers. Choose the correct word for each space (1-9).
For each question, mark the letter next to the correct word — A, B, C or D. There's
an example at the beginning (0).

Caesar was very (0) ...*good*.......... at winning the favour of his soldiers
(1) .... the common people of Rome. Before the civil war between Pompey
and him, Caesar gave large amounts of money to his soldiers. He gave them even
(2) .... after his victory. Caesar then gave grain, oil and money to the
people of Rome. Caesar also won the favour of the poorer people of Rome by paying
their rent. He also put on great shows (3) .... entertain the people. For
example, he began the combat of gladiators in the city. He also put on plays in
different parts of the city and in different languages. (4) .... of the shows
were truly magnificent. For example, wild animals (5) .... hunted

(6) .... five days in the stadiums. These animals included elephants, camels and lions. After this, they put on representations of battles with twenty elephants on each side. A sea battle was even represented for the people. To (7) .... this, they made a large artificial lake. (8) .... public entertainments were very popular and people even came from outside the city to see them; they put up tents in the streets of Rome.

The crowds were (9) .... large that a number of people were even crushed to death, including two senators.

0	(A) good	B well	C capable	D expert
1	A also	B too	C and	D but
2	A more	B much	C lot	D many
3	A at	B for	C so	D to
4	A some	B any	C number	D every
5	A was	B are	C be	D were
6	A to	B since	C at	D for
7	A make	B give	C do	D put
8	A those	B the	C these	D them
9	A much	B so	C very	D really

4 Summary

Choose the correct word in brackets to make a complete summary of Parts Three-Four.

The night before the assassination, Brutus could not sleep. His **1** *(wife/mother/sister)*, Portia, came to him and asked him what he was worried about. At first he didn't tell her. Then she showed him a wound on her **2** *(hand/leg/arm)*. She had done it herself to show Brutus that she was brave. Brutus then told her his secret. Caesar, too, did not sleep that night. His wife Calpurnia told him that the **3** *(gods/people/senators)* were angry. She also told him about her **4** *(poem/story/dream)* in which the Romans washed their hands in Caesar's **5** *(wine/water/blood)*. Caesar also heard about the strange results of a sacrifice: the animal had no **6** *(heart/stomach/blood)*.

In the morning, Decius, one of the conspirators, came to accompany Caesar to the Senate House. But now Caesar was frightened and wanted to stay home. Finally, Decius convinced him to go.

When they arrived in front of the Senate House, a man named Artemidorus gave Caesar a letter that told about the conspiracy. But Caesar refused to read it and entered the Senate House.

When he was inside, the conspirators came up to Caesar. Casca was the first to stab him. The last to stab Caesar was **7** *(Cassius/Decius/Brutus)*.

Later at Caesar's funeral Brutus spoke to the Roman people. He told them that he loved Caesar but loved Rome more. He had killed Caesar because Caesar wanted to become **8** (rich/senator/king).

Then Mark Antony spoke to the crowd. He never really **9** (mentioned/accused/celebrated) Brutus, but he showed that Caesar was not really **10** (ambitious/powerful/dangerous). Finally, he showed the people Caesar's **11** (will/picture/letter). After this speech, the people of Rome wanted to **12** (help/kill/know) all of the conspirators.

Listening activity: the questions can be found online at www.blackcat-cideb.com. Go to the *Julius Caesar* page.

Before you read

1 Listening

PET
You will hear about the preparations for war after the assassination of Caesar. For each question, put a tick (✓) in the correct box.

1 The people of Rome
  A ☐ were not interested in Antony.
  B ☐ were on Antony's side.
  C ☐ were against Antony.

2 Octavius came to Rome
  A ☐ just before Caesar was killed.
  B ☐ several months before Caesar was killed.
  C ☐ just after Caesar was killed.

3 If they won the war against Brutus, Octavius, Lepidus and Antony would
  A ☐ each have part of Caesar's money.
  B ☐ each have part of the Empire.
  C ☐ each have part of the army.

4 Antony thought that everybody who agreed with the conspiracy should
  A ☐ leave Rome.
  B ☐ be killed.
  C ☐ pay money.

5 Antony agreed that his nephew should die because
  A ☐ he did not want to appear weak.
  B ☐ he was afraid of Lepidus.
  C ☐ he did not like his nephew.

PART FIVE

PREPARATIONS FOR WAR

Antony now had the support of the people of Rome. The conspirators had run away from the city. Antony remembered the promise he had made over the body of his friend.

'Caesar's spirit will have revenge', he said to himself. 'Brutus and his friends will die!'

Caesar's nephew, Octavius, arrived in Rome soon after the death of the great man. He, too, wanted revenge for the death of his uncle. Octavius and Antony agreed to work together, and they asked Lepidus to join them.

The three men planned to raise [1] a great army, and to fight against the army of Brutus and his friends. They agreed to divide the Roman Empire between them after they had defeated Brutus.

'Before we fight,' Octavius said, 'we must decide what to do about the Romans who supported the conspiracy. There are some people in the city who knew about the conspiracy. They did not help Caesar. They are traitors, as well!'

---

1.   **raise** : bring together.

Julius Caesar

'You're right,' said Antony. 'Let's make a list of these men. We'll execute [1] them all!'

'Execute them all, Antony?' asked Lepidus. 'Are you sure that you want to execute them all?'

'They must all die,' Antony said firmly. [2] He did not really want to kill his nephew, but he knew that he had to show Lepidus that he was strong. 'Even my own nephew, Publius, must die. Your brother must die as well, Lepidus. They are both traitors.'

'I agree,' Lepidus said. 'We will put my brother and your nephew on the list of people to die.'

Lepidus was a good soldier. Octavius and Antony needed his help with their army. But Antony did not want to share the Roman Empire with Lepidus. He did not respect him.

'Lepidus is a good soldier, I admit,' Antony said to Octavius. 'But that's all he is. I know we have offered to divide the Empire with him — but is that really necessary, do you think?'

'We promised,' Octavius replied. 'He is a brave man, and he is loyal.'

'He's a stupid man,' Antony said. 'Let's wait until we defeat Brutus. Then we won't need Lepidus any more. We can divide the Empire between the two of us — it will be better!'

'Do what you want,' Octavius told him. 'We mustn't argue now. The important thing now is to defeat Brutus and his army.'

Brutus and Cassius were also busy. They had decided to raise two different armies. Cassius was in control of one army, and Brutus was in control of the other army. They wanted to bring both of their armies together, to fight against Octavius, Antony and Lepidus.

The two men did not see each other until they brought the two armies together. They had written letters while they were apart, but the friendship between them was beginning to change.

'You have not been fair to me, Brutus,' Cassius complained. 'You punished Lucius Pella. When I wrote to you about him, you ignored my letter. Lucius Pella was a good friend of ours!'

---

1. **execute** : kill.
2. **firmly** : decisively.

'A good friend!' Brutus replied. 'He was not honest with money. I punished him for his dishonesty.'

'You don't understand,' Cassius replied. 'I need a lot of money to pay for my army — Lucius Pella helped me to find that money. He was a good friend, I tell you!'

Brutus looked at his friend with surprise.

'Cassius, Cassius,' he said sadly. 'What has happened to you? We killed Caesar because we believed in justice, didn't we? Our cause is a noble one — we must be noble, too! Otherwise, why did we kill Caesar?'

'Again I tell you, you don't understand, Brutus. My army needs money. I take money when people offer it to me.'

Brutus began to be angry now.

'You like money too much, Cassius. That's your problem!'

'Be careful, Brutus! No one can say that about me — not even you. I am a soldier. Remember that!'

'I'm not afraid of you, Cassius. I'm tired of you. You're a bad man. You're not even a good friend.'

'What's happening to us, Brutus?' Cassius asked. 'Once we were good friends. Now you don't want my friendship any more. You don't like me.'

'I don't like your faults, Cassius,' Brutus told him.

Cassius was very sad. He admired Brutus. He could not bear [1] to lose Brutus's friendship. He took out his knife, and gave it to Brutus.

'Kill me, Brutus,' he ordered. 'Kill me, as you killed Caesar. I know that you loved Caesar more than you ever loved me,' he said sadly.

'Put away the knife,' Brutus said kindly. 'I know you are my friend. I spoke when I was angry, but now I am not angry. Forgive me, my friend.'

'I never thought you would talk to me like that,' Cassius said.

'I am very sad, my friend,' Brutus told him. 'Portia is dead.'

'Portia dead! How did it happen?' Cassius asked.

'She was worried about me,' Brutus explained. 'She heard about the great army that Antony and Octavius have made. She became ill, and she killed herself.'

---

1. **could not bear** : hated.

Julius Caesar

Cassius was very shocked. The two friends looked at each other in silence for a while.

Then Brutus and Cassius spoke about their plans for war. They knew that Antony and Octavius had a large army. They were leading their army towards Philippi. Brutus wanted to march to Philippi at once, but Cassius disagreed.

'It's better to stay where we are,' he said to Brutus. 'If Antony and Octavius bring their army to us, their soldiers will be tired when they arrive. Our chances of victory will be greater.'

'I don't agree,' Brutus said. 'I think we should march to Philippi. We have a good cause. Our army is ready to fight. Let's go to Philippi, and defeat the enemy!'

'Very well,' Cassius said. 'If you want to take the army to Philippi, that is what we will do.'

It was now late at night, and Brutus was tired. He wanted to sleep.

'We'll meet in the morning, Cassius my friend,' he said. 'Now we need rest.'

Cassius left his friend. Brutus picked up a book, and began to read. He read for a few minutes. Then he thought he heard a noise. He looked up, and there in front of him, he saw the ghost of Caesar!

'You!' he cried. 'Why are you here?'

'I have a message for you,' the ghost announced.

'Message? What message?'

The ghost stared at Brutus.

'You will see me again — at Philippi,' it said. Then it disappeared.

The text and **beyond**

PET **1 Comprehension check**

Look at the statements below about Part Five. Decide if each statement is correct or incorrect. If it is correct, mark A. If it is not correct, mark B.

A B

1 Antony wanted Brutus to be killed. ☐ ☐
2 Antony thought that only the conspirators should be killed. ☐ ☐
3 Antony did not want to have Lepidus on his side in the fight against Brutus. ☐ ☐
4 Brutus and Cassius each had their own soldiers. ☐ ☐
5 Cassius got money for his army dishonestly. ☐ ☐
6 Cassius wanted to die because he thought Brutus was no longer his friend. ☐ ☐
7 Brutus spoke badly to Cassius because he was afraid. ☐ ☐
8 Portia became ill because she was afraid for her husband. ☐ ☐
9 Brutus thought it would be easier to win at Philippi. ☐ ☐
10 The ghost of Caesar told Brutus that it would be present at the battle. ☐ ☐

2 Vocabulary

Historians say that Caesar was a great general, leader and speaker. Caesar also made many reforms. Do the puzzle below and discover one of his reforms that still touches our lives today. The answer will appear vertically.
Write the opposite of the words below. All the words come from Part Five.

1 put down
2 small
3 hated
4 forgot
5 began
6 intelligent
7 birth
8 opposed

1 ☐☐☐☐☐☐ ☐☐
2 ☐☐☐☐☐
3 ☐☐☐☐☐
4 ☐☐☐☐☐☐☐☐☐☐
5 ☐☐☐☐☐
6 ☐☐☐☐☐☐☐
7 ☐☐☐☐☐☐
8 ☐☐☐☐☐☐☐☐☐

3 Discussion

Brutus says that has killed Caesar for freedom. But already he accuses Cassius of corruption.
In the end, the main result of the assassination seems to be civil war and violence. With your partner discuss the following points, and then present your ideas to the class.

1 Can violence ever bring justice?
2 Can you think of any war or revolution that was originally fought for justice, but which caused only violence and suffering.

They must all die

In the text you read: 'They *must* all die,' Antony said firmly. 'Even my own nephew, Publius, *must* die. Your brother *must* die as well, Lepidus. They are both traitors.' (Antony agrees that the deaths of these people are necessary.)

Must is used to indicate that the speaker thinks it is necessary to do something.

In the text you read: 'Do what you want,' Octavius told him. 'We *mustn't* argue now. The important thing now is to defeat Brutus and his army.' (Octavius says that it is necessary for Antony and him not to disagree.)

Must not is used to indicate that the speaker thinks it is necessary not to do something.

'You *needn't* make a list of the traitors', Octavius told them. 'I can remember them all.'

(Octavius says that it is unnecessary to make a list.)

Need not (needn't) is used to indicate that the speaker thinks it is unnecessary to do something.

4 Must or must not
Complete the sentences below with *must* or *must not*.

1 Caesar was afraid to go to the Senate House. Decius thinks, 'I .... convince him to come.'

2 Artemidorus gives Caesar a letter and says to him, 'You .... read it now!'

3 Caesar thinks, 'Who is this man anyway? He .... tell Caesar what to do!'

4 When Caesar was first stabbed he was frightened, but then he said to himself, 'You .... be frightened. You are Caesar.'

5 Mark Antony believes that all the traitors .... be executed.

6 Mark Antony also believes that he and Lepidus .... make exceptions for their family.

5 Complete the sentences below with *must not* or *need not* (needn't).

1 Portia says to Brutus, 'I am very worried about you.' Brutus answers, 'You .... worry about me. I'm only a little ill.'

2 Calpurnia says to Caesar, 'You .... go to the Senate House. People saw lions in the streets of Rome.'

3 Brutus says to Cassius, 'You .... do dishonest things.'

4 Portia says to her slave, 'You .... bring me my dinner. I'm too worried about my husband to eat.'

5 Brutus says to Cassius, 'You .... be hurt by my words. I didn't mean them. I am only sad for the death of Portia.'

The Romans in Britain

The first Roman invasion of Britain – led by Julius Caesar - took place in 54 BCE. This was not a major invasion of all of Britain because Caesar was busy fighting in Gaul (modern France) at the time. After some victories against tribes in the south of Britain, the Romans soon left.

Nearly one hundred years later, in 43 CE, the emperor Claudius organised another invasion of Britain, this time a major one. Four Roman legions landed in Kent, in the south-east. In three years the Romans had conquered the south of Britain and most of the central area.

But the conquest of Britain was not easy for the Roman invaders. In 60 CE, the queen of the Iceni tribe, Boudicca, who had been treated very badly by the Romans, led a revolt against them. Boudicca's army successfully attacked and destroyed the new Roman towns at Colchester, London and St Albans before

being heavily defeated by the Roman Governor Suetonius Paulinus.

Over the next forty years the Roman presence in Britain became stronger: the Roman army moved into Wales and defeated the tribes there and they moved into northern England, and defeated the local tribe there, the Brigantes.

Bust of the **Emperor Hadrian** (about 135 CE).
Under Hadrian the Roman empire was at its biggest.

Remains of **Hadrian's Wall** can still be seen and visited today.

The Romans also invaded the northern part of Britain, which they called Caledonia and is now called Scotland, where the general Agricola defeated the inhabitants, the Caledones, at the battle of Mons Graupius. The Caledones continued the war against the Romans, however, and in 100 CE the Romans left this part of Britain. In 122 CE the emperor Hadrian visited Britain. The Romans decided that they could not defeat the Caledones, and so they built a huge wall between the two parts of the country.

The Romans remained in England until 410 CE, when the soldiers in Britain had to go to other parts of the Empire which were being invaded. During their stay in Britain the Romans built towns and roads and established schools and a legal system. The name Britain comes from the Roman name for the island, Britannia.

▶▶▶ INTERNET PROJECT ◀◀◀

Go to the Internet and go to www.blackcat-cideb.com or www.cideb.it.
Insert the title or part of the title of the book into our search engine.
Open the page to *Julius Caesar*. Click on the Internet project link.
Scroll down the page until you find the title of this book and click on the relevant link for this project.
Work in pairs or small groups. Find out more about the Roman invasion of Britain and about Roman life. Choose one of the topics below and explore the website. Prepare a short oral presentation for the rest of the class about what you find out. You can use images from the website if you want.

- ▶ The Roman invasion of Britain
- ▶ Leisure activities
- ▶ Roads
- ▶ The Roman army
- ▶ Religion
- ▶ Towns and homes
- ▶ Food

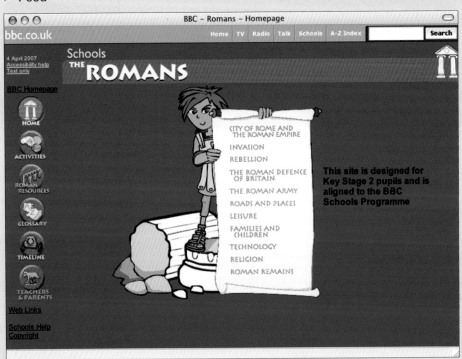

Well-known Roman sites in Britain

- Hadrian's Wall: originally built at the time of the emperor Hadrian, the wall was subsequently destroyed and rebuilt. It extends for about 70 miles (112.6 kilometres) across the north of the country, from the east coast to the west coast.
- Bath Roman Museum: the Roman baths in the city of Bath in south-west England are an example of how the Romans brought public baths to Britain.
- Bignor Roman Villa: these remains in the south-east of England contain some beautiful mosaics.
- Fishbourne Roman Palace: this site is believed to be the palace of a British king, Cogidubnus, who became 'Romanised'. It contains mosaics and a Roman-style garden.

The **Roman bath** in the city of Bath:
the English city took its name from the presence of the bath.

INTERNET PROJECT

Go to the Internet and go to www.blackcat-cideb.com or www.cideb.it .
Insert the title or part of the title of the book into our search engine.
Open the page to *Julius Caesar*. Click on the Internet project link.
Scroll down the page until you find the title of this book and click on
the relevant link for this project.

As you have read, the museum in Bath, called Aquae Sulis by the Romans, is
one of the most popular Roman sites in Britain. The thermal baths were popular
with the ancient Romans.

First find out how to get there by train or car.

In pairs or small groups, research one of the following topics. Present a report to
the class, along with some pictures from the Internet site.

▶ What was the religious nature of the Roman baths?

▶ What were the baths like in Roman times?

▶ When were the Roman baths discovered in modern times?

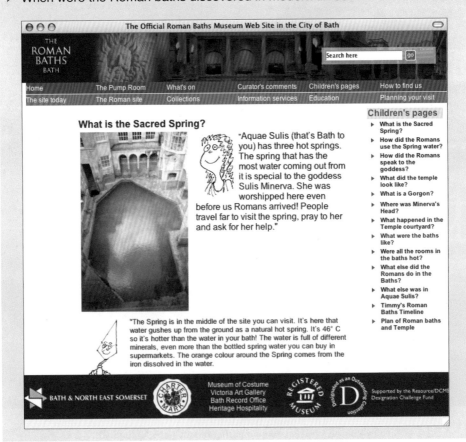

PET ◆① Comprehension check

How much can you remember about the Roman invasion of Britain? For each question, choose the correct answer — A, B, C or D.

1 Julius Caesar
    A ☐ did not conquer Britain.
    B ☐ conquered some of Britain.
    C ☐ conquered all of Britain.
    D ☐ conquered all of Britain, but then lost it.

2 Boudicca
    A ☐ defeated the Romans and became queen of Britain.
    B ☐ defeated the Romans in numerous battles, but was then defeated.
    C ☐ never defeated the Romans in any battles.
    D ☐ defeated other tribes who helped the Romans.

3 The Romans built Hadrian's Wall to
    A ☐ celebrate their victory over the Caledones.
    B ☐ keep the Caledones out of Roman Britain.
    C ☐ protect their armies in their battles against the Caledones.
    D ☐ protect the Iceni tribe against the Caledones.

4 The Romans were in Britain for about
    A ☐ 500 years.   C ☐ 400 years.
    B ☐ 200 years.   D ☐ 300 years.

▶11 Listening activity: the questions can be found online at www.blackcat-cideb.com. Go to the *Julius Caesar* page.

Before you read

▶12 **① Listening**

PET ◆

Look at the six sentences below. You will hear about the beginning of the battle between Caesar's friends and Caesar's enemies. Decide if each sentence is correct or incorrect. If it is correct, put a tick (✓) in the box under A for YES. If it is not correct, put a tick (✓) in the box under B for NO.

	A YES	B NO
1 The four generals decided to meet after the battle began.	☐	☐
2 Brutus thought fighting was always better than talking.	☐	☐
3 Cassius told the others to stop talking and begin fighting.	☐	☐
4 Cassius was certain of victory.	☐	☐
5 Cassius and Brutus felt sad.	☐	☐
6 Cassius and Brutus went to fight together against Antony.	☐	☐

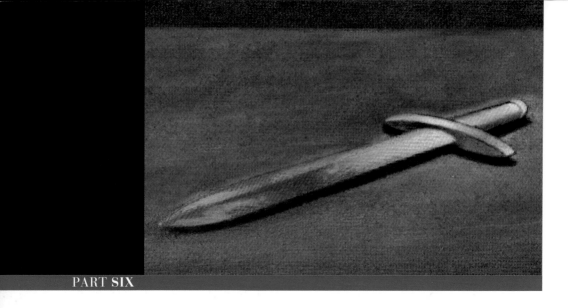

PART SIX

THE DEATH OF CASSIUS

The army of Brutus and Cassius marched to Philippi, where they found the army of Antony and Octavius. The four generals decided to meet each other before they gave the command to fight. Both armies faced[1] each other as the leaders talked.

Brutus was the first to speak.

'You want to exchange words before we exchange blows,[2] is that right?'

'We know that you like to talk, Brutus,' Octavius said angrily.

'Sometimes it is better to talk than to fight,' Brutus replied.

'We know the value of your words, Brutus,' said Antony. 'You said Caesar was your friend, and then you stabbed him!'

'And we know the value of your words, Antony,' Cassius said angrily. 'You promised us friendship, and then you raised an army against us!'

'Enough words!' cried Octavius. 'I didn't come here to talk — I came here to kill traitors!'

---

1. **faced** : stood opposite.

2. **exchange blows** : fight.

The generals returned to their armies.

Brutus and Cassius spoke together before the battle began. Cassius was serious and thoughtful. He had doubts about the battle, and he mentioned these to Brutus.

'If we lose today, what will you do?' he asked.

'We will win today, or we will die,' Brutus said. 'When we killed Caesar, we started something that will end today.'

The two friends looked sadly at each other for a moment.

'Let's say goodbye to each other now,' Brutus suggested. 'We may never see each other again.'

Cassius said goodbye to his friend, and then he went back to his part of the army. He felt sad, and he was worried about the battle. He knew that the enemy was strong.

The fighting was hard for Cassius and his men. They were brave, but so were Antony's men. It seemed that Antony's men would defeat Cassius's part of the army. Some of Cassius's soldiers wanted to run away from the battle. Cassius thought that the battle was going badly. He spoke to one of his officers.

'Our men are frightened, Titinius. Some of them have run away from the enemy. We're in trouble!'

'Brutus has attacked Octavius's men too soon,' Titinius said. 'He should have waited.'

Just then Cassius's servant, Pindarus, joined them.

'Antony's men have defeated us, Cassius — we've been defeated!'

'And Brutus — what's happening to Brutus?' Cassius wanted to know. 'Get on your horse, Titinius, and ride to his part of the army. Find out how the battle is going there.'

Cassius and Pindarus watched as Titinius rode away. Titinius rode very fast, but there was soon a group of men around him. Titinius could not ride any further, and he stopped his horse.

'He's a prisoner!' Pindarus shouted to Cassius. 'The enemy have taken him. Listen to them shout!'

Suddenly Cassius was afraid.

'We will lose,' he cried. 'The enemy is too strong for us!'

He called Pindarus to him.

'You have served me well, my friend,' he said. 'Now there is one final thing I ask you. We have lost the battle. There is no future for me. Either I must be Antony's prisoner, or I must die. I prefer to die. I used this sword when we

killed Caesar. Take it, and kill me with it.'

Pindarus took Cassius's sword.

'Caesar has his revenge!' cried Cassius. He ran onto the sword, and died.

Pindarus was wrong when he said that Titinius was a prisoner.

Julius Caesar

The group of men around him were from Brutus's part of the army. They were shouting because they were happy. Brutus had defeated Octavius's men.

'Cassius will be pleased with the good news,' Titinius told them. 'I'll ride back to tell him the battle is going well.'

Titinius rode towards the place where he had left Cassius. There was no one there. He looked everywhere for his friend. He discovered his body lying on the ground.

'My poor friend!' he cried. 'You have died for nothing — we were winning!'

Titinius took Cassius's sword, and killed himself with it.

The news that Cassius and Titinius were dead made Brutus very sad. 'Another revenge for Caesar!' he thought.

'Carry their bodies away,' he instructed some soldiers. 'They were the best of all the Romans. Cassius, my good Cassius,' he went on 'your death is terrible to me. I will find time to remember you, I will find time.' Then he turned to the soldiers again. 'Now we must finish the battle,' he ordered.

The text and **beyond**

1 Comprehension check

The four generals argue about 'words' when they meet before the battle. Use the chart below to show what Antony says about Brutus, and what Cassius says about Antony.

	Antony's view of Brutus
What Brutus says	
What Brutus does	
	Cassius's view of Antony
What Antony says	
What Antony does	

Cassius sends Titinius to Brutus's part of the army. He wants to find out how the battle is going. Complete the chart below with the following information:

What Pindarus sees	What Pindarus assumes	The real situation

Why does Cassius kill himself?

2 Caesar and the pirates

Plutarchus (46-127 CE), the Greek philosopher and biographer, wrote the famous *Lives of the Noble Greeks and Romans*, also known as *Parallel Lives*. This book contains biographies of famous ancient Greeks and Romans in pairs. For example, Julius Caesar is paired with the Greek king and conqueror Alexander the Great (356-323 BCE). In his biography of Caesar, Plutarch tells about when Caesar was captured by pirates in 75 BCE.

PET Look at the statements about Caesar and the pirates. Read the text below to decide if each statement is correct or incorrect. If it is correct, mark A. If it is not correct, mark B.

		A	B
1	Caesar wanted the pirates to know how important he was.	☐	☐
2	Caesar wanted to be friends with the pirates.	☐	☐
3	The pirates did not like Caesar's poems.	☐	☐
4	The pirates did not think Caesar really wanted to execute them.	☐	☐
5	The pirates finally received the 50 talents of gold.	☐	☐
6	Caesar wanted to have revenge on the pirates.	☐	☐
7	Caesar told his men to kill the pirates in a slow, painful way.	☐	☐

After Caesar was captured by the pirates, their leader came to Caesar and said, 'We are going to ask for 20 talents [1] of gold for your ransom [2].' Caesar laughed at him and said, 'You don't know who I am. Twenty talents? That's ridiculous, I myself will pay you 50 talents!'

The pirates were shocked, but happy. Caesar sent some of his men to obtain the 50 talents of gold.

Now these pirates were the cruellest and most dangerous men in the world, but Caesar treated them like servants. If they made noise at night, Caesar would shout, 'Be quiet! I need to sleep.'

Caesar was a prisoner of the pirates for 38 days, but he did not seem at all worried or frightened. He joined the pirates in all their games and sports. Sometimes he wrote poems and speeches, and read them to the pirates. 'Well, what do you think of my speech,' Caesar asked the pirates. The pirates did not understand much and could only say, 'Oh, well... very nice.' Caesar would become angry and shout, 'You ignorant fools! You understand nothing!'

Other times, Caesar laughed and in a playful way said, 'When I am freed, my men will crucify [3] all of you!'

The pirates were surprised by Caesar's attitude and words. To explain them, they said, 'This Caesar is simple and playful like a young boy.'

In the end, Caesar's ransom was paid, and he was freed. Caesar then immediately took some ships and went and captured the pirates. And, just as Caesar promised, all the pirates were crucified. But, before they were crucified, Caesar's men cut the pirates' throats. So, the pirates were already dead when they were crucified. This was very kind of Caesar because crucifixion was a long and horrible way to die.

1. **talent** : about 40 kilos; an ancient measure of weight.
2. **ransom** : money paid to free a prisoner.
3. **crucify** : to execute by nailing a person to a cross.

Antony's men have defeated us, Cassius – we've been defeated!

Compare these two sentences:

The soothsayer **has sacrificed** the cow. (active)
The cow **has been sacrificed** by the soothsayer. (passive)

The second sentence focuses on the cow and what has happened to it.
The passive is often used to change the emphasis of a sentence.

Notice that *by* says who did something in a passive sentence.

3 **Present Perfect Passive**
Change the following sentences into the passive form.

1 The people of Rome have attacked the conspirators.
2 Antony has defeated the enemy.
3 Someone has killed Caesar.
4 The lion has eaten a citizen.
5 Calpurnia has asked Caesar not to go to the Senate.

Change the following sentences into the active form (the subject of the active sentence is given in brackets).

1 He's just been made king by the senate.
2 A letter explaining the conspiracy has been written by Artemidorus.
3 Caesar has been captured by pirates.
4 Caesar has been stabbed by Brutus.
5 Caesar has been warned about the Ides of March by the soothsayer.

13 Listening activity: the questions can be found online at www.blackcat-cideb.com. Go to the *Julius Caesar* page.

Before you read

14 **1** **Listening**
Listen to the beginning of Part Seven. For each question, fill in the missing information in the numbered space.

Brutus led his men (**1**) .... to the fighting. They were all unhappy about Cassius's (**2**) ...., but he tried to give them courage. The soldiers liked Brutus very much, and they wanted to win the (**3**) .... for him.
One of the young soldiers was the (**4**) .... of Marcus Cato.
'Come on, men!' he cried. 'I'm not (**5**) .... of the enemy.' He marched into the enemy, calling out, 'I'm Cato — I'm fighting for (**6**) ....!'
The enemy (**7**) .... saw the young Cato, and they (**8**) .... him.

73

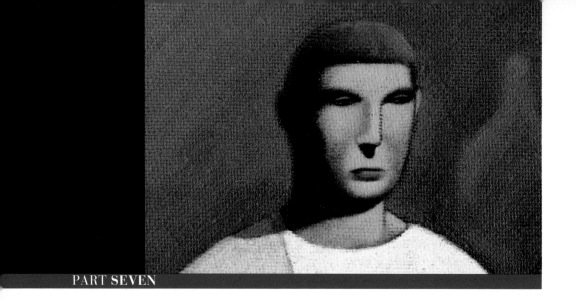

PART **SEVEN**

THE DEATH OF BRUTUS

Brutus led his men back to the fighting. They were all unhappy about
Cassius's death, but he tried to give them courage. The soldiers liked Brutus
very much, and they wanted to win the battle for him. One of the young
soldiers was the son of Marcus Cato.

'Come on, men!' he cried. 'I'm not afraid of the enemy.' He marched into
the enemy, calling out, 'I'm Cato — I'm fighting for freedom!'

The enemy soldiers saw the young Cato, and they killed him.

Lucilius saw the young Cato die.

'I'll save Brutus from the enemy,' he thought. 'I'll pretend to be Brutus. The
enemy will kill me, but they will not kill Brutus.' He, too, marched into the
enemy. He called out, 'I'm Brutus, my country's friend — kill me if you can!'

The enemy soldiers saw Lucilius. They believed that he was Brutus. They
captured him, and took him to Antony.

'We've taken Brutus,' they told Antony. 'He's our prisoner.'

Antony looked at the soldiers and their prisoner.

'Where is he? Where's Brutus?' he asked.

'Brutus is not here,' Lucilius said. 'Your soldiers will never take Brutus,
Antony. He loves freedom too much to be a prisoner.'

THE DEATH OF BRUTUS

'This is not Brutus,' Antony told his soldiers. 'This is Lucilius, a friend of Brutus. Lucilius is trying to save his friend's life.'

Brutus's soldiers fought very hard, but the army of Antony and Octavius was stronger. Many of Brutus's friends were killed. Now Brutus knew that the battle was lost.

'Caesar has won,' he thought. 'I will die today.'

He called his friends to him.

'We will rest here for a moment,' he said.

Then he turned to one of the men with him, and asked him something in a low voice.

'I can't do it, Brutus — I can't do that!' Clitus replied. 'Ask me anything, but not that.'

Brutus turned to another friend, and asked him the same thing.

'No, Brutus, no!' Dardanius said. 'It's impossible.'

Clitus spoke to Dardanius.

'I saw that Brutus asked you something. What did he ask you to do?'

'He asked me to kill him,' Dardanius said. 'But I refused to do it.'

'He asked me, as well,' Clitus said. 'I refused as well.'

Brutus called another friend, Volumnius.

'Last night I saw the ghost of Caesar again,' he said. 'Our army is beaten. I must die today. Help me to die, Volumnius, my friend.'

'I can't help you to die, Brutus,' Volumnius told him. 'You're my friend.'

Brutus looked at the soldiers around him. He could hear the shouts of the enemy soldiers. There was not much time left.

'Farewell [1] to all of you,' he said. 'You have all been loyal to our cause, and I thank you.'

'The enemy is coming, Brutus!' cried Clitus. 'Run, Brutus, run!'

The soldiers began to run from the dangerous place.

'Go! Save yourselves, my friends!' Brutus ordered his men. 'I will stay here for a moment longer. Strato, stay with me — I want you to do something for me.'

Soon Brutus and Strato were alone.

---

1. **Farewell** : Goodbye.

'The enemy are coming,' Brutus said. 'I don't want to be a prisoner. Hold my sword for me, Strato — hold it, and let me run on it, as Cassius ran on his sword.'

Strato held Brutus's sword.

'Caesar, you have won, at last!' cried Brutus. Then he ran onto his sword.

Antony and Octavius arrived with their soldiers. They saw the body of Brutus.

'What happened?' Antony asked Strato.

'Brutus wanted to die,' Strato told them. 'I held his sword for him.'

Antony looked at the body of his enemy.

'He was the best man of all the conspirators,' he said. 'All of them hated Caesar. They killed him because they were frightened of him. Brutus was different. He killed Caesar because he loved Rome. Brutus was a noble man!'

The text and **beyond**

1 Comprehension check

Who said what and why? Match the quotes with the character who said them, and then match the quotes with the reasons why they said them. You can use some characters more than once.

WHO

Antony (A)   Brutus (B)   Dardanius (D)   Lucilius (L)   Cato (C)

1 ☐ ☐ 'I'm not afraid of the enemy.'

2 ☐ ☐ 'I'm Brutus, my country's friend.'

3 ☐ ☐ 'Brutus is not here.'

4 ☐ ☐ 'This is not Brutus.'

5 ☐ ☐ 'Caesar has won.'

6 ☐ ☐ 'It's impossible.'

7 ☐ ☐ 'I don't want to be a prisoner.'

8 ☐ ☐ 'Brutus was different.'

A He realizes that Antony will win the battle.

B He is refusing to help his friend kill himself.

C He is telling his enemies that he has tricked them.

D He is trying to give the other soldiers the courage to win the battle.

E He is honouring his dead enemy.

F He is explaining why he wants to kill himself.

G He is explaining to his men who their prisoner is.

H He is sacrificing himself for Brutus.

2 Writing

Revenge is Mine

Pretend you are Julius Caesar, and in 100-150 words say how, in the end, you won. Include the following information:

• how Rome greeted you after your victory
• how you reacted to the offer of the crown
• what the soothsayer said
• who killed you
• Cassius's great mistake
• your revenge

You can begin like this:

I am the great Julius Caesar and, in the end, revenge is mine! It all began after my victory over Pompey. The great city of Rome ...

3 Summary

Number the paragraphs below in the right order to make a summary of Parts Five-
Seven. Then fill in the gaps with the words in the box.

Philippi	fought	revenge	ran	ghost	refused	
raised (x2)	brave	executed	battle	defeated	noble	
won	shouts	led	conspiracy	march	prisoner	loved

A ☐ Soon Cassius lost all hope. He did not want to be Antony's **(1)** ...., so he asked his friend Pindarus to kill him.

B ☐ The night before they left, Brutus saw the **(2)** .... of Caesar. It told him that he would see it again at **(3)** .... and then it disappeared.

C ☐ Finally, the **(4)** .... began between the great armies. The men on both sides were **(5)** ...., but Cassius's army began to lose to Antony's army.

D ☐ Finally, Brutus heard the **(6)** .... of the enemy. His men began to run away. Brutus then convinced Strato to hold his sword. Brutus **(7)** .... into it and died. Then Antony and Octavius arrived and saw the body of Brutus.

E ☐ Brutus was very sad when he received the news of his friend's death. But he still **(8)** .... his men to battle. They **(9)** .... very hard but the enemy was stronger.

F ☐ Brutus then knew that Caesar had **(10)** ...., and that he would die. He asked his friends to kill him, but they **(11)** ....

G ☐ When Brutus and Cassius heard about the armies of their enemies, they too **(12)** .... armies. However, they each had different ideas about fighting the war. Cassius wanted to wait for his enemies to come, and Brutus wanted to **(13)** .... to Philippi. In the end, they decided to follow Brutus's plan.

H 1 After the assassination, the conspirators ran away. Antony promised **(14)** .... for the death of Caesar. He **(15)** .... armies with Octavius and Lepidus. They also **(16)** .... all the people who had supported the **(17)** ...., even their own relatives.

I ☐ Antony then said that Brutus was a **(18)** .... man who killed Caesar because he **(19)** .... Rome.

J ☐ But Cassius died for nothing. All was not lost: Brutus had **(20)** .... some of Octavius's forces.

🔊 Listening activity: the questions can be found online at www.blackcat-cideb.com.
Go to the *Julius Caesar* page.

Shakespeare's *Roman Plays*

The tragedies of the Roman playwright Seneca (4 BCE-65 CE) were very influential in the second half of the 16th century. Many playwrights tried to copy Seneca's themes and style, and 'Roman tragedies' were popular with audiences. Many dramatists wrote plays with typically 'Roman' themes concerned with honour, nobility and patriotism… and a lot of blood.

In his own Roman tragedies, Shakespeare uses the history of 'great men' to explore the relationship between public character and the individual. His source for the plots of his Roman plays was a translation made in 1579 by Sir Thomas North of the *Lives of the Noble Grecians and Romans* by the Greek historian Plutarchus (46-127 CE).

Remains of a **Roman theatre** in Leptis Magna on the coast of Libya.

A scene in the Senate House from the film **Julius Caesar** directed by Joseph Mankiewicz (1953). The American actor Marlon Brando won the best actor Oscar for his role as Mark Antony.

- *Julius Caesar* is a political drama. It raises questions about the relationship between a leader and the people. It shows how a political idealist like Brutus can make bad decisions, such as letting Antony speak at Caesar's funeral. As well as being a political drama, *Julius Caesar* is also a drama about character. In the scenes involving Calpurnia and Portia, Shakespeare goes behind the public behaviour of the major characters to reveal their private relationships.

- *Antony and Cleopatra* continues the story of Mark Antony's life, after his arrival in Egypt and love affair with Cleopatra, the Egyptian queen. In this play private emotions are shown to be stronger than political ambition and judgement.

- In *Coriolanus* the protagonist, the nobleman Coriolanus, needs the support of the Roman people in order to fulfil his ambitions, but he is too proud to ask for that support.

PET 1 Comprehension check

For each question, choose the correct answer — A, B, C or D.

1 Roman tragedies were
   A ☐ copied by English playwrights.
   B ☐ not known in Shakespeare's time.
   C ☐ not very popular in Shakespeare's time.
   D ☐ not understood in Shakespeare's time.

2 Shakespeare got the stories for his Roman plays from
   A ☐ a translation of Seneca.
   B ☐ other English playwrights.
   C ☐ the writings of Julius Caesar.
   D ☐ a translation of Plutarchus.

3 Julius Caesar is a political drama because it
   A ☐ explains how Roman government worked.
   B ☐ focuses on the relationship between a leader and the people.
   C ☐ shows the private behaviour of political figures.
   D ☐ explains the ideas behind Roman government institutions.

4 Antony and Cleopatra is a play about
   A ☐ the conflict between private emotions and political ambitions.
   B ☐ politics and revenge.
   C ☐ how politics destroys private lives.
   D ☐ the differences between Roman and Egyptian societies.

5 Coriolanus is about
   A ☐ the protagonist's problems with his family.
   B ☐ the history of Rome.
   C ☐ the protagonist's dilemma about needing the Roman people's help.
   D ☐ the conflict between the army and the Roman Senate.

2 Rome in books, films and television

What novels have you read, or what films or TV series have you seen that were set in ancient Rome? Make a list in class. Which are the most popular, and why?

▶▶▶ INTERNET PROJECT ◀◀◀

Go to the Internet and go to www.blackcat-cideb.com or www.cideb.it.
Insert the title or part of the title of the book into our search engine.
Open the page to *Julius Caesar*. Click on the Internet project link.
Scroll down the page until you find the title of this book and click on the relevant link for this project.

Cleopatra has been a favourite of the stage ever since Shakespeare wrote *Antony and Cleopatra*. Find out more about the stage costumes for Cleopatra over the years. Present a short report to the class.

1 What did the real Cleopatra look like?
2 How did she dress?
3 How has the Cleopatra costume changed over the years?
4 Was the costume used in Shakespeare's time historically accurate?
5 Download two or three pictures you like and explain them to the class.

PET ③ Orson Welles: the genius of American film and theatre

Look at the statements below about one of America's most famous film and theatrical directors. Read the text below to decide if each statement is correct or incorrect. If it is correct, mark A. If it is not correct, mark B.

		A	B
1	At the end of his life Welles was most famous for his innovative work in radio, theatre and film.	☐	☐
2	The manager of the Gate Theatre didn't care that Welles lied to him.	☐	☐
3	Welles eliminated all scenes with magic from *Macbeth*.	☐	☐
4	Welles made Brutus into a modern character.	☐	☐
5	Brutus, in Welles's version of *Julius Caesar*, became a kind of a Fascist.	☐	☐
6	After Welles, nobody used *Julius Caesar* to talk about the contemporary world.	☐	☐
7	Welles tricked many people with his version of *The War of the Worlds*.	☐	☐
8	Welles presented *The War of the Worlds* as if it were a radio news programme.	☐	☐
9	Welles used many new ideas in making *Citizen Kane*.	☐	☐
10	Welles made many films for Hollywood studios after *Citizen Kane*.	☐	☐
11	*Citizen Kane* did not make much money.	☐	☐

In the 1970s most Americans knew who Orson Welles (1915-85) was: he was that fat man with a beard who appeared in a television ad for the Paul Masson wine company. This was certainly a strange destiny.

Sadly, both of Orson Welles's parents died when he was young. Despite this, Welles was a confident young man. When he was only 16, he walked into the Gate Theatre in Dublin and told the manager that he was an American star. The manager didn't believe him, but he gave him a role in a play anyway. Welles was a big success.

A photograph of **Orson Welles** taken in about 1939.

When he was 20, Welles directed Shakespeare's tragedy *Macbeth* for the American Negro Theatre of New York. He did it in a very innovative way: he set this Scottish play of witches and magic in Haiti with its voodoo ceremonies. It was a huge hit.

Welles then started his own company of actors, the Mercury Theatre. His 1937 version of Shakespeare's *Julius Caesar* was set in Fascist Italy and all the actors wore uniforms much like those worn by the Fascists and Nazis. Brutus represented the ideals of the democratic countries of the time. Welles also cut out large sections of the play, eliminated characters and even added dialogue from other plays. One of the most famous changes involved the death of Cinna the poet. In the original play Cinna was killed by an angry crowd of people; in Welles's version he was killed by the secret police force. Many people liked Welles's version very much. Others, though, said that Welles had made Shakespeare's tragedy too superficial. In any case, many later productions of *Julius Caesar* followed Welles's example and made clear references to contemporary political events.

But perhaps Welles's most exciting work was his adaptation of the science-fiction novel *The War of the Worlds* by H. G. Wells (1866-1946). On 30 October 1938 Welles presented this radio play as if it were a real radio news programme. It had a normal introduction as a radio play, but many people did not hear the introduction. In fact, Welles knew that most of the public listened to another more popular show, and then changed stations during the advertisements — just as we do today while watching television. So, many people believed that Martians had actually landed in the United States, and the radio station received thousands of telephone calls from terrified listeners. Welles later said that he was sorry that people took his radio play so seriously. However, few people believed him: 30 October - the day before Halloween - in the USA, Canada and the United Kingdom is called Mischief Night: it is the night when many young people play different tricks on their neighbours.

Now Welles was very famous and the Hollywood film studios gave him an incredible opportunity: Welles could direct a major film and control every part of its production. This film was called *Citizen Kane* and it came out in 1941. This film was inspired by the life of the newspaper magnate William Randolph Hearst (1863-1951). However, Hearst did not like this film at all, and he made certain that it was not a financial success. But now it is often considered one of the greatest and most innovative films ever made.

Welles continued to work in theatre and film, but after *Citizen Kane* he was never again accepted by the major Hollywood film studios. In fact, Welles often had difficulty getting money for his projects. In the end, America's genius of film and theatre was most famous for selling wines.

1 Suetonius's account of the assassination and funeral of Julius Caesar
Read this short version of the description by the Roman historian Suetonius of the
assassination and funeral of Julius Caesar. Suetonius's descriptions of these
events are generally considered the most accurate.
Then find four things in Suetonius's account that are the same or similar to
Shakespeare's play, and four things that are different. Then find three things that
are not mentioned in Shakespeare's play.

Different

a   Calpurnia dreamt that their house fell down and that Caesar was stabbed in her
    arms.
b   ....
c   ....
d   ....

The same

a   The conspirators planned to kill Caesar in the Senate House.
b   ....
c   ....
d   ....

Not mentioned

a   One of the signs telling of the assassination of Caesar was the horses crying
    and not eating.
b   ....
c   ....

The conspirators finally agreed to kill Caesar in the Senate House on the Ides of
March. Before this date there were many signs warning of Caesar's assassination.
For example, Caesar had freed some horses to celebrate his victory over Pompey,
and now these horses refused to eat and began to cry abundantly. Also a
soothsayer told Caesar to be careful of a great danger on the Ides of March.
The night before the assassination, Calpurnia, Caesar's wife, dreamt that their
house fell down and that Caesar was stabbed in her arms. So, the next day Caesar
did not want to go to the Senate, but Decius, one of the conspirators, convinced him
to go.
When he entered the Senate someone gave him a note revealing the conspiracy.
Caesar took it and planned to read it later. When he saw the soothsayer he laughed
and said, 'You were wrong. It is the Ides of March and nothing has happened.' The
soothsayer responded, 'Yes, they have come, but they not yet gone.'
When Caesar was seated in the Senate House, Cimber approached him to ask him
something and then held him. Casca stabbed him first. In the end he was stabbed 23
times and did not say a word.

Mark Antony spoke at Caesar's funeral. But he only said that the Senate had given Caesar many honours, and had promised to protect him.

Then the great fire was lit to burn Caesar's body. In honour of Caesar, people threw different things into the fire: his soldiers threw in their arms, and women threw in their jewellery and the clothing of their children.

PET ❷ Comprehension check

For each question, choose the correct answer — A, B, C or D.

1 Caesar fought and won a war against
   A ☐ Cassius.
   B ☐ Casca.
   C ☐ Pompey.
   D ☐ Brutus.

2 Caesar wanted Antony to touch Calpurnia because it would
   A ☐ help him defeat his enemies.
   B ☐ bring him and his wife money.
   C ☐ help him be a good ruler of Rome.
   D ☐ help Calpurnia have children.

3 The people applauded Caesar at the feast of Lupercal because
   A ☐ he promised to give them money.
   B ☐ he had defeated Pompey.
   C ☐ he refused the crown.
   D ☐ he said he wanted to be king.

4 Cassius said that the lion walking the streets of Rome meant that
   A ☐ Caesar was going to be a good and powerful king.
   B ☐ Caesar represented a great danger for Rome.
   C ☐ Caesar was going to be killed by powerful men.
   D ☐ Caesar needed to be strong to rule Rome well.

5 Caesar was surprised that among the conspirators there was also
   A ☐ Cassius.
   B ☐ Brutus.
   C ☐ Casca.
   D ☐ Metellus Cimber.

6 How did Antony show the Roman people that Caesar loved them?
   A ☐ He showed them Caesar's will.
   B ☐ He told them that Caesar wanted to be a good king for them.
   C ☐ He told them that Caesar protected them from bad men like Cassius.
   D ☐ He read them a speech Caesar had written for them.

7 Antony decided that his nephew must die because his nephew

A ☐ did not want to fight against Brutus.

B ☐ was part of the conspiracy to kill Caesar.

C ☐ knew about the conspiracy but didn't help Caesar.

D ☐ did not want Caesar to become king.

8 Brutus punished Cassius's friend Lucius Pella because he

A ☐ was against the conspiracy.

B ☐ would not give Brutus any money.

C ☐ did not want to fight in Brutus's army.

D ☐ was not honest with money.

9 Cassius killed himself because he

A ☐ finally realized it was wrong to kill Caesar.

B ☐ he thought Brutus was no longer his friend.

C ☐ he did not want to become Antony's prisoner.

D ☐ he was sad about the death of Portia.

10 Lucilius pretended to be Brutus to

A ☐ save Brutus's life.

B ☐ save his own life.

C ☐ approach Cassius.

D ☐ confuse Brutus's army.

3 Writing

Read this comment:

'*Julius Caesar* is about people in ancient Rome over two thousand years ago. It may be an interesting story, but it is not relevant to today's world.'

Write a short essay (about 150-200 words) in which you agree or disagree with the comment above.

Key to Exit Test

1 Different

b Caesar did not say a word while he was being attacked.

c Caesar was given a note inside the Senate House.

d Mark Antony only says that the Senate promised to protect Caesar.

The same

b They planned to kill Caesar on the Ides of March.

c A soothsayer warned Caesar

d Decius convinced Caesar to go to the Senate house.

Not mentioned

b He was stabbed 23 times.

c Caesar was burnt.

2 1 C; 2 D; 3 C; 4 B; 5 B; 6 A; 7 C; 8 D; 9 C; 10 A

3 Open answer.

Julius Caesar

Playscript

ACT ONE

A street in Rome. Flavius and Marullus are talking to some of the citizens.

MARULLUS: What are you doing here? You should be at work today. It's not a public holiday.

CITIZEN: I've come to see Caesar, sir. There's a big procession in his honour. I want to see it. He's defeated his enemies. It's a great day for Rome.

FLAVIUS: A great day for Rome, is it? Caesar has defeated Pompey's sons. You cheered for Pompey once, didn't you? Now you're cheering Caesar!

MARULLUS: You should go home, good people.

CITIZEN: Perhaps we will, sir.

ACT TWO

A street in Rome. Cassius and Brutus are talking.

CASSIUS: Brutus, I'd like to speak to you for a minute.

BRUTUS: What is it, Cassius?

CASSIUS: You've been ignoring your friends lately, Brutus. What's the matter?

BRUTUS: Nothing, Cassius — nothing at all. I've been thinking a lot recently, that's all. But I haven't forgotten my old friends, you can be sure of that.

CASSIUS: I'm glad to hear it, Brutus, because Rome needs a man like you. We want someone who will...

Julius Caesar

A shout from the area where the race is taking place.

BRUTUS: I wonder what that was! I hope they're not offering Caesar the crown.

CASSIUS: Then you don't want Caesar to be king, Brutus?

BRUTUS: No, Cassius, I don't want Caesar to be king. I don't think anyone should be king. Rome doesn't need kings.

Another shout from the area where the race is taking place.

CASSIUS: I agree with you. Caesar's just an ordinary man, like you and me. Why should he be king? He's not even particularly strong or brave. We were soldiers together, you know. I remember once when he was ill, he cried out for water like a child. And another time, he challenged me to swim across the Tiber with him. He got halfway across, then he called out 'Help me, Cassius! Help me!' I don't want him to be king.

BRUTUS: Perhaps they will make him king — I know Antony wants to offer him the crown.

Another shout from the area where the race is taking place.

BRUTUS: Let's ask someone what's going on. Look, there's Casca — let's ask him. Casca! Casca!

CASCA: Yes, what is it? What can I do for you, Brutus?

BRUTUS: What's happening in there? What's going on?

CASCA: It's a silly business, Brutus. Antony offered Caesar a crown.

BRUTUS: Did Caesar take it? Did he refuse?

CASCA: He refused it the first time, and the people cheered.

CASSIUS: And then what happened?

CASCA: Then Antony offered it to him again. He refused again, and the people cheered again.

BRUTUS: We heard three shouts, Casca. What was the last shout for?

CASCA: The same thing, Brutus. Antony offered him the crown a third time, and he refused it again. He wanted to take it, but he couldn't, you see. The people cheered when he refused it. So he had to go on refusing it. But if you ask me, that man wants to be king — he wants it badly!

Julius Caesar

ACT THREE

The same night, a storm in Rome.

CASCA: Who's that?

CASSIUS: It's a friend, Casca.

CASCA: It's you, is it, Cassius? What a terrible night this is. I've been walking up and down, and I've seen some strange things in the city tonight. There's a lion in the streets. The gods are angry with Rome, Cassius. The gods are very angry.

CASSIUS: I don't agree with you. I don't think the gods are angry with Rome. I think these strange things have a different meaning. That lion you saw, Casca. There's a man in the city who reminds me of a lion. A man who terrifies everybody.

CASCA: You mean Caesar, don't you? I hear the Senate are going to offer him the crown again tomorrow morning. He's sure to take it this time. It looks as if Rome is going to have a king after all, my friend.

CASSIUS: I carry a knife with me. I'll die if I have to, but I'll never live under tyranny.

CASCA: I'm the same. I'll die if I have to, but I'll die a free man.

CASSIUS: But it isn't us who have to die, Casca... it's that lion that has to die.

CASCA: I see what you mean. You think we should kill Caesar. That's it, isn't it?

CASSIUS: There are other men in the city who think like you and me, Casca. Why don't you come along later tonight, and meet some of them. We need a man like you.

CASCA: All right, I will.

Casca leaves Cassius on stage alone.

CASSIUS: It's going well. More people join the conspiracy every day. But we need Brutus to join, as well. The people respect him. I'll go and see him later tonight.

Julius Caesar

The middle of the night. Brutus is in the garden of his house. He is alone.

BRUTUS: Caesar's dangerous, I'm convinced of that. If he becomes king, we'll all lose our freedom. But he's my friend — I don't want to kill him. But freedom is more important than the life of a man — more important than the life of a friend, even. I'll join this conspiracy!

A knock at the door. The servant brings in the conspirators.

BRUTUS: Welcome, Cassius. Welcome to you all!
CASSIUS: You know why we are here, Brutus. We must make a plan for tomorrow morning. We have to stop Caesar before he becomes king.
BRUTUS: We must act tomorrow. Caesar must die tomorrow in the Senate House.
CASSIUS: What about Antony? I think we should kill him, as well. He's a dangerous man. He likes Caesar, and he will be our enemy.
BRUTUS: I don't agree with you, Cassius. Without Caesar, Antony's not dangerous at all. Besides, if we kill him, the people will think we're just murderers. I say we should let him live.
CONSPIRATOR: Brutus is right. Antony's no danger to us.

ACT FIVE

The next morning at the Senate House. Caesar is surrounded by the conspirators.

CAESAR: Who wants to ask the advice of Caesar and the Senate?
METELLUS CIMBER: I do, great Caesar. I ask you to let my brother come back to Rome, Caesar.
CAESAR: I banished Publius Cimber. You know that I never change my mind. Publius Cimber will not come back to Rome!
CONSPIRATORS: We also ask for his return, great Caesar!

CAESAR: I will not listen to you — I have decided this matter.

BRUTUS: I also ask for the return of Publius Cimber.

CASCA: Now!

Casca stabs Caesar. The other conspirators stab him as well. He struggles for a while, until he sees Brutus with his knife ready to kill him.

CAESAR: Even you, Brutus?

Caesar dies.

BRUTUS: Think, my friends, this is a great moment in history. In the future, when we are all dead, actors will play the death of Caesar in front of audiences. No one will ever forget what we have done today!

The conspirators talk among themselves.

BRUTUS: Let's go into the centre of the city! Let's tell the people of Rome what we've done. Let's tell them why Caesar had to die.

Brutus addressing the people in the centre of Rome.

BRUTUS: Caesar was my friend, but I love Rome more than I loved Caesar. And I love freedom more than I loved Caesar. I killed Caesar because he was ambitious. He wanted to be king. He wanted to take away our freedom.

CITIZEN 1: We want Brutus to be our leader! Brutus for king!

BRUTUS: Antony is here. He was Caesar's friend, as well. He wants to speak to you. Please listen to what he says. He speaks with my permission.

CITIZEN 2: We don't want to hear Antony! We want to hear Brutus!

BRUTUS: Please listen to what Antony says.

ANTONY: Friends, Romans! Brutus has told you that Caesar was ambitious, and Brutus is an honourable man. But I want to ask you something. Caesar made Rome rich with his victories — was that ambitious of him? I offered him the crown at the feast of Lupercal, and he refused it. He refused it three times — was that ambitious of him? Was Caesar ambitious then?

CITIZEN 3: That's right, he did refuse the crown. I was there. I saw him refuse the crown. He didn't want to be king!

Julius Caesar

ANTONY: Brutus is an honourable man. All the conspirators are honourable men. I don't want to argue with them. I can only tell you this. You don't know how much Caesar loved you! I've got his will here.

CITIZENS: Read the will! We want to hear the will! Read the will!

ANTONY: Caesar left every Roman citizen a piece of money. He left his gardens to the people of Rome, as well. He was a great man, and he loved you all!

CITIZENS: It's true, Caesar was a great man. Brutus and his friends are murderers and traitors. We'll kill them — we'll kill them all!

ACT SIX

Before the battle at Philippi.

BRUTUS: You want to exchange words before we exchange blows, is that right, Antony?

OCTAVIUS: We know how you like fine words, Brutus.

BRUTUS: Talking is better than fighting sometimes.

ANTONY: And you're such a talker, aren't you, Brutus? You talked about Caesar as if he were your friend — but you killed him, all the same!

CASSIUS: And you, Antony? You talked about giving us your friendship, and then you raised an army against us.

OCTAVIUS: I didn't come here to talk to traitors. I came here to revenge Caesar's death.

During the battle. Cassius's part of the army.

CASSIUS: Our men are frightened. Some of them have run away. I fear that we will lose this battle, Titinius.

TITINIUS: Brutus has attacked too soon. He should have waited.

PINDARUS: Antony's soldiers are winning, sir!

CASSIUS: Go to Brutus. Find out how the battle is going there. Ride quickly!

TITINIUS: Yes, Cassius — I'll go immediately.

Titinius rides away.

CASSIUS: What's happening now? What's Titinius doing?

PINDARUS: The enemy has surrounded him. They've stopped his horse. They've taken him prisoner!

CASSIUS: We'll lose the battle. The enemy is too strong for us. But I will never be a prisoner. Help me to die, Pindarus.

Pindarus holds his sword, and Cassius runs onto it.

CASSIUS: Caesar is revenged!

Cassius dies. Titinius returns. He sees the body of Cassius on the ground.

TITINIUS: O Cassius, my poor friend. You have died for nothing — we were winning! They were not enemy soldiers you saw — they were friends.

Titinius also kills himself. Enter Brutus and friends.

BRUTUS: Cassius was my friend, and I will weep for him. We have lost the battle, and it is time for me to die. Who will help me to die? You, Clitus?

CLITUS: No, Brutus, no! I'm your friend — I'll never help to kill you.

BRUTUS: You, Dardanius? Will you help me to die?

DARDANIUS: I will not, Brutus.

CLITUS: The enemy's coming. Run, save yourselves!

BRUTUS: Go, all of you. I will stay here a while. Strato, stay here with me for a moment.

Brutus and Strato are alone on stage.

BRUTUS: I will never be a prisoner, Strato. Hold my sword for me, I beg you.

Strato holds Brutus's sword, and he runs onto it. Enter Antony.

ANTONY: Brutus was the noblest Roman of all the conspirators. All of them, except Brutus, killed Caesar because they were frightened of him. But Brutus did it because he believed that Caesar was dangerous for Rome.

This reader uses the **EXPANSIVE READING** approach, where the text becomes a springboard to improve language skills and to explore historical background, cultural connections and other topics suggested by the text.

The new structures introduced in this step of our **READING & TRAINING** series are listed below. Naturally, structures from lower steps are included too. For a complete list of structures used over all the six steps, see *The Black Cat Guide to Graded Readers*, which is also downloadable at no cost from our website, www.blackcat-cideb.com or www.cideb.it.

The vocabulary used at each step is carefully checked against vocabulary lists used for internationally recognised examinations.

Step **Three** **B1.2**

All the structures used in the previous levels, plus the following:

Verb tenses
Present Perfect Simple: unfinished past with *for* or *since* (duration form)
Past Perfect Simple: narrative

Verb forms and patterns
Regular verbs and all irregular verbs in current English
Causative: *have / get* + object + past participle
Reported questions and orders with *ask* and *tell*

Modal verbs
Would: hypothesis
Would rather: preference
Should (present and future reference): moral obligation
Ought to (present and future reference): moral obligation
Used to: past habits and states

Types of clause
2nd Conditional: *if* + past, *would(n't)*
Zero, 1st and 2nd conditionals with *unless*
Non-defining relative clauses with *who* and *where*
Clauses of result: *so*; *so ... that*; *such ... that*
Clauses of concession: *although, though*

Other
Comparison: *(not) as / so ... as*; *(not) ... enough to*; *too ... to*

Available at Step **Three**:

- **The £1,000,000 Banknote** Mark Twain
- **The Canterville Ghost** Oscar Wilde
- **Classic Detective Stories**
- **The Diamond as Big as The Ritz** F. Scott Fitzgerald
- **Great Mysteries of Our World** Gina D. B. Clemen
- **Gulliver's Travels** Jonathan Swift
- **The Hound of the Baskervilles** Sir Arthur Conan Doyle
- **Jane Eyre** Charlotte Brontë
- **Kim** Rudyard Kipling
- **Lord Arthur Savile's Crime and Other Stories** Oscar Wilde
- **Moonfleet** John Meade Falkner
- **Of Mice and Men** John Steinbeck
- **The Pearl** John Steinbeck
- **The Phantom of the Opera** Gaston Leroux
- **The Prisoner of Zenda** Anthony Hope
- **The Return of Sherlock Holmes** Sir Arthur Conan Doyle
- **The Scarlet Pimpernel** Baroness Orczy
- **Sherlock Holmes Investigates** Sir Arthur Conan Doyle
- **Stories of Suspense** Nathaniel Hawthorne
- **The Strange Case of Dr Jekyll and Mr Hyde** Robert Louis Stevenson
- **Tales of the Supernatural**
- **Three Men in a Boat** Jerome K. Jerome
- **Treasure Island** Robert Louis Stevenson
- **True Adventure Stories** Peter Foreman

READING SHAKESPEARE

- **Julius Caesar**
- **Romeo and Juliet**
- **Twelfth Night**